Are We There Yet?
Author: Mitch Triestman

Lifeline Publications
19 Primrose Lane
Levittown Pa. 19054
215 945 3277

foibs@aol.com

Third Printing

Other Lifeline Publications

To the Jew First – By Mitch Triestman. A textbook on Jewish evangelism with an exhaustive section on apologetics.

Abraham, the Committed Christian – By Mitch Triestman. Both a devotional book for believers and a clear message of the gospel for unbelievers.

When Loved Ones are Taken in Death – By Dr. Lehman Strauss. Messages of hope and comfort in time of sorrow.

Are We There Yet?

Author: Mitch Triestman

Copyright © 2016 by Mitch Triestman

Printed in the United States of American for
19 Primrose Lane
Levittown, PA 19054
215-945-3277

Printed by H.G. Publishing
Langhorne, Pennsylvania 19047

The views expressed in this work are those of the author.
The author is solely responsible for its contents.

All rights reserved.

No portion of this book may be reproduced in any form without written permission of the author, except in the form of brief quotations embodied in critical articles or reviews.

Library of Congress Control Number: 2015960168
ISBN 978-0-9801037-9-3

Contents

CHAPTER 1   How To Be Good Looking 1

CHAPTER 2   One Taken, One Left 17

CHAPTER 3   Signs 47

CHAPTER 4   Seven Prophetic P's 99

CHAPTER 5   Jacob's Trouble 119

CHAPTER 6   The Great White Throne 147

ENDNOTES 159

Are We There Yet?

Introduction

I just returned home from a speaking engagement at a local church. After the service several people recommended that I write a book on Bible prophecy. I thought that my expert presentation had provoked them to further study and the folks were desirous of a book to assist them. Actually my presentation was so completely disjointed that these good folks recommended that I try writing, since it was painfully obvious that public speaking was not my gifted area. Scores of excellent books are already in print on the subject. This volume will not add anything new in the way of information or insight. However, after a sermon folks desire to study the material they just heard. I often speak too fast and offer this book as a service to those who had to endure the preaching. This book is only an attempt to enhance the ministry of the pulpit.

My burden is to see Jewish people come under the influence of the Gospel. Understanding prophecy will reveal the unique position and importance of Israel. The purpose of this book is to shame you, shock you and shake you into the witness to God's ancient people that you ought to be. The proceeds will enable us to give a copy of "Abraham the Committed Christian" to an unsaved Jewish person. So if you don't reach the Jewish people with the Gospel, perhaps Abraham might.

CHAPTER ONE

How To Be Good Looking

People are obsessed over appearances. Reality takes a back seat to perception. We are far more concerned about how we look, than how we are. If cigarettes caused pimples, people would not smoke. Cigarettes cause cancer, which is invisible to the unassisted eye. In the Hebrew Scriptures we were given a uniform to wear, so that the entire nation of Israel might look alike. In the Greek Scriptures we are not told what we should look like, we are told what we are to look for.

To help us look in the right direction, we like to begin a series on prophecy by telling the story of the rabbi on the moped. Two men were sitting in a very fancy and expensive sports car, at a traffic light, when a rabbi on a moped pulled up next to them. The men looked over at the rabbi condescendingly. The driver stepped down on the accelerator. He revved up the powerful engine **Vroom! Vroom!** And in doing so extended a challenge to the rabbi. The rabbi stared at the costly and impressive machine and accepted the challenge by revving up the tiny motor on his bicycle **Ying, Ying, Ying!** The light turned green and the men nailed their respective machines.

The rabbi pulled out to the early lead and went through all five gears in about fifteen feet, **Ying, Ying, Ying, Ying, Ying!** The sports car then lurched into motion and quickly left the rabbi in the dust. They looked up in the rear view mirror and then slowed down to see if there was any trace of the rabbi. As they looked back, the driver tapped the brakes trying to allow the rabbi to catch up a bit. Suddenly they saw a little black dot in the mirror. The dot loomed larger and larger and then grew life size. Something flashed abruptly by them, **whoosh**, on the right hand side of the car and as soon as it appeared, it disappeared beyond the horizon.

"What was that?"

"I don't know!"

They questioned their eyes as the driver accelerated and tried to catch up with whatever it was that has just raced on ahead.

There in front of them they saw that little black dot. Again it grew larger and larger and loomed life size and unexpectedly pushed past the sports car, **whoosh**, going in the opposite direction. They questioned each other and their own eyes, then slowed down and looked back only to see that little black dot again. The black dot started to grow as it drew closer to them and one more time it raced past their fancy sports car and disappeared in front of their vehicle.

"I think that was the rabbi!"

"On the moped? How can that be?"

"I don't know?"

They continued to question each other as the driver accelerated and for a second time tried to catch up with the black dot that had once more vanished in front of them.

Just as before, the black dot grew life size as it drew near them and for a final time, it pushed past them going in the other direction. **Whoosh!**

"I saw him, it was the rabbi!"

"On the moped? How can that be?"

"I have no idea."

This time the driver stopped the sports car to get a better perspective on the fast-moving, direction-changing moped. That little black dot re-appeared in the mirror and all over again it grew larger and larger as it drew nearer to the sports car. Now, instead of racing by them, the rabbi on the moped smashed into the rear end of the car. They heard the crashing of glass and all kinds of clangs and bangs and terrible sounds. The two men jumped out of the car to see if the rabbi had been hurt.

They said, "Rabbi are you alright? What can we do to help?"

The rabbi responded with, "Well if you can be so kind as to unhook my suspenders from your fender, I would appreciate it."

Usually when I tell that silly story I get a few chuckles. One of our other missionaries would tell the same story and no one ever laughed. We discovered that his rabbi was holding his pants up with a belt and it just did not work. I tell the story to get people to look around, to look back and to look ahead. I do not believe that anyone can fully appreciate prophecy without proper appreciation of history.

Looking Back

We have recently had many well-known and respected Bible teachers making silly statements about Biblical prophecy. The date setting crowd has made a mockery of serious Bible study in the area of eschatology[1]. Currently the church tends to view any study in the field with suspicion. Many believers think prophecy to be a spurious endeavor. To escape criticism, pastors are abandoning the field and prophetic messages are disappearing from our pulpits. Some are circling their wagons within the camp that teaches that all prophetic texts are symbolic and spiritual and have no literal way of being understood. It is a safe position to claim that prophecy is filled with symbolism and that it is of no value to attempt to make literal sense of the texts. It is without risk to say that it all will pan out in the end. We will never err if we venture no interpretation.

Too many believers have lost the true meaning and sense of purpose in this life as a result of this thinking and preaching. Ignorance of prophecy has caused us to make the error of the misguided servant in Luke 12:45, who thought to himself that his master was delaying his return and began to live as if the master did not matter. The prophetic message keeps us focused on the eternal and encourages us to diminish the temporal. Without a prophetic focus we fall easily into the trap of living this life as if it were our only life. Good looking is to keep looking up, for our redemption is drawing near. However, to be truly good looking, we need to look back before we can look forward.

I hear messages that challenge congregations on the basis of the "soon coming of Jesus." I just do not get the point. One pastor talked about the Lord coming back and catching us in bars or movie theaters. The Holy Spirit of the Living God lives within us. When we go into bars and movie theaters, we take the Holy Spirit with us. That presence and the message of God's love should prove to be the deterrent that we need. No, I do not think the prophetic message should serve as a restraint. God stood by His love for us and while we were yet sinners, He sent His son to die for us. Sir Isaac Watts, in response to that love, wrote in the hymn, "When I Survey the Wondrous Cross":

> *Were the whole realm of nature mine,*
> *That were a present far too small:*
> *Love so amazing, so divine,*
> *Demands my soul, my life, my all*

That should provide all the necessary motivation for a life of obedience. Looking back reminds us of God's great love. Looking back at Jesus also teaches us how to be good looking when we look forward. The Gospel stands in the framework of prophecy. 1 Corinthians 15:1-3 says Christ died for our sins according to the Old Testament Scriptures. From Daniel 9:26 we discover who is central to the gospel when we read that, *"the Messiah will be cut off."* In Isaiah

53:8 we learn why He was cut off when we read, *"he was cut off out of the land of the living: for the transgression of my people was he stricken"*.

He was buried according to Isaiah 53:9 and rose again (Psalm 16:10) on the third day (Hosea 6:2). The virgin birth is prophesied in Isaiah 7:14 and the place of the Messiah's birth, the city of Bethlehem, is prophesied in Micah 5:2. Jesus is verified by prophecy. His life, His death, His ministry, His credentials were authenticated on the basis of prophecy, fulfilled literally and historically.

Jesus also made predictions. He predicted the destruction of the Temple (Matthew 24:2). The significance of that Temple cannot be overly stressed. It was a political icon that stood as evidence of the grandeur of the realm of Herod the great. The magnificent architectural structure testified to the wealth and ability of the society that could develop it; a pinnacle of architectural splendor for the Roman world. As a religious structure, it was positioned at the center of the Jewish world. All Jewish males must make pilgrimage to it three times every year. Its very existence declared the reality of the Creator whose presence met with His creation within her sacred walls. The Jewish people considered it to be the very core of the entire universe; the center of Jewish religious life. The destruction of the Temple seemed ludicrous. It just could not happen. Yet the unthinkable occurred. In 70 A.D., the Romans entered the city of Jerusalem and destroyed the Temple, which remains demolished to this day.

In contrast to the ultimate destruction of the Temple, Jesus predicts His own resurrection (John 2:19). With reference to His body, Jesus said they could destroy *"this Temple"* and in three days He would raise it up. These two predictions were fulfilled literally and historically. We can travel to the land of Israel and see the geography that declares the method of interpreting Biblical prophecy. The Temple is indeed in ruins and the tomb is empty.

The ruined Temple and the empty tomb stand in a geographical location as visual instructional aides. The ruined temple teaches us that there is no place on earth where a further offering can be brought. The lifeless Temple lying in rubble shows a dead religious system. The bad news of the temple is counteracted by the good news of the empty tomb. The empty tomb shows that the sacrifice offered on behalf of our sins has been accepted. It teaches us that we can stand *"holy and unblameable and unreproveable in his sight"* Colossians 1:22. Together, the tomb and the Temple combine to teach us that Bible prophecy is to be interpreted literally first and needs not to be spiritualized.

Looking Forward

Good looking forward is looking for prophecy to be fulfilled in a literal manner. In 1 Thessalonians 4:16-17 Paul teaches us how *"the Lord Himself will descend from heaven with a shout, with the voice of an archangel, and with the trumpet of God. And the dead in Christ will rise first. Then we who are alive and remain shall be caught up together with them in the clouds to meet the Lord in the air. And thus we shall always be with the Lord."* This event is what has traditionally been referred to as the "rapture."[2]

The rapture is a hotly debated issue. The big question is when will the rapture occur. Because it has become a divisive subject, some have opted to choose a path of peace. They take a pseudo-spiritual posture and tragically refuse to study the subject. Others deny that the rapture will occur at all. They teach that there is one and only one general resurrection from the dead and then the judgment.

Paul tells the Thessalonians to comfort one another with the message about the rapture. They had apparently expressed concerns about their departed loved ones. The news that those who sleep will be raised is only part of the comfort. The real comfort comes from the information *"We who are alive and remain shall...meet the Lord in the air."* (1Thess 4:17)

Paul mentions the appearance of the Lord Himself, the announcing shout, the archangel's voice, the alarming trumpet, the arising dead, the ascent of the living and the assembly in the air. The Apostle Paul does not mention six trumpet judgments; he makes no mention of the six seals. He does not refer to the restored nation of Israel, the ten-nation dynasty, the one world religion and the universal economic system. He does not write about the beast, the false prophet, nor the 144,000. Paul believed and taught that the next event was the resurrection of the church and that event could take place during his lifetime.

Good looking is to be looking for Jesus. Titus 2:13 reads, *"Looking for that blessed hope and the glorious appearing of our great God and Saviour Jesus Christ."* 1 Thessalonians 1:10 reads, *"And to wait for his Son from heaven, whom He raised from the dead, even Jesus who delivers us from the wrath to come."* In James 5:7 we are admonished to be patient unto the coming of the Lord. James continues to mention the early and the later rain, which is a cryptic reference to both the first and second advents.[3] James 5:8 reads, *"You also be patient. Establish your hearts, for the coming of the Lord is at hand."* Hebrews 10:37 reads, *"For yet a little while and he who is coming will come, and will not tarry."* The Apostle who wrote the book of Hebrews believed in the imminent return of the Lord Jesus. James believed in the imminent return of the Lord Jesus. Paul believed and taught the imminent return of Jesus. Today, Bible teachers are smarter than the Apostles.

Today, many teach that the resurrection at the end of the tribulation[4] is the rapture. If the rapture occurs at the end of the tribulation, then we must wait seven years for Jesus to return and the return of Jesus cannot be imminent. If the rapture occurs in the middle of the tribulation, then we must look for the antichrist, the Seal Judgments and the tribulation events and we become bad looking. The return of Jesus is no longer imminent and the church suffers because of sloppy Biblical thinking in this arena.

Are We There Yet?

In the first chapter of Acts, when the disciples ask the resurrected Lord if He was now going to establish the kingdom, the Lord refused to give them a direct answer. It was a simple yes or no question that would normally call for a yes or no answer. Instead, Jesus said that it is not in their power to know, and that they would receive power after the Holy Spirit would come upon them and that they would be His witnesses. But He refused to answer the question. He could not say yes because that was not true. He was not about to set up the kingdom. He could have said no, but He chose instead to ignore the question.

Our church frequently schedules short-term missionary trips for our youth and others. The folks who take advantage of these opportunities come back electrified. Each morning they start the day with prayer and Bible studies. They spend the days in genuine tasks and ministries, which assist the missionaries. In the evenings, they share the answers to prayer and the blessings of the day. They live exciting lives of active service for two full weeks. They are pumped and when they share their testimony with the congregation, they pump us all up. However, after two weeks, they return to their daily routines. It seems that we are capable of making total commitments to God for only brief periods of time.

This may be the reason why Jesus refused to answer the question in the first chapter of the book of Acts. Jesus could have said, "No! I am not going to set up the kingdom for thousands of years. You will all live and die on this earth and so will your children and their children for generation after generation."

I think that if Jesus had answered the question in such a manner he would have discouraged the early church from being the world changing dynamic witness it was in the first century. These early Christians sold all their possessions and placed the proceeds at the feet of the Apostles. They had all things in common. They continued steadfastly in the Apostle's doctrine and in prayers. *"Breaking bread from house to house... the Lord added to the church daily those who were being saved."* (Acts 3:46-47)

This first century church became the witness for Jesus in Jerusalem, in Judea and when driven out by persecution, became the martyred witness to the outermost parts of the World. Those believers made a dynamic commitment to their God and King on the basis of history, but they were encouraged to live out that commitment with enthusiasm in the belief that Jesus could return any moment. The expectation of an imminent return provides the source for energy, passion and dedication.

I heard of a game called "Mack truck." Teens play it while on weekend retreats and during overnight camp programs. The game calls for three players and one person, a contestant, upon whom the game is played. The three players require some special equipment. One player needs a loud air horn; the kind that blast at outdoor sporting events. The second player is equipped with two bright halogen lamps, while the third player needs a large bed pillow. The contestant only needs to drift off into REM[5].

Just as the contestant begins to fall asleep, the three players sneak quietly up and strategically place themselves around the bed. The one with the air horn stands directly over the contestant's ears. The player with the lamps stands at the foot of the bed, while the player with the pillow is positioned about waist high. Then the players wield their respective tools. The air horn is blasted first and the two bright lamps are immediately snapped on right behind it.

If the timing is right the illusion is amazing. Upon hearing the horn the contestant opens his eyes and stares directly into what will appear to be headlights. The contestant instinctively sits up and that is when the player armed with the pillow comes into action. He will smack the contestant back down completing the impression. The contestant heard the horn, saw the lights and imagined that he was about to be run over by a Mack truck. When the pillow smashes him in the face, he knows he has been run over by the truck. It is a teenage stress test. No person over thirty has ever been a contestant and survived.

Are We There Yet?

I am told that the contestant is up and awake for the duration of the camp program. The adrenaline is pumping through his veins and he will not be able to sleep for days. This pumping of adrenaline is what prophecy is supposed to do for us. When we start looking for anything else to happen before or besides the return of Jesus, we become lethargic in our Christian walk. When we cease to be good looking, we need to be roused. I want to blow a horn in your ear, shine a light in your eyes and smack you over the head with a pillow. I want to wake you out of your trance and make you realize that the trumpet could sound at any second.

Troublesome times are here, filling men's hearts with fear.
Freedoms we all hold dear,
Now are at stake.

Humble your hearts to God, save from the chastening rod.
Seek the path Pilgrims trod.
Christians awake!

Jesus is coming soon! Morning or night or noon
Many will meet their doom.
Trumpets will sound.

All of the dead shall rise. Righteous meet in the skies
Going where no one dies,
Heavenward bound[6].

From the first time I heard that song I loved the message but disagreed with one line. We cannot say with certainty that Jesus is coming soon. We must assert with all surety that Jesus can come at any moment. We do live in exciting and challenging times and we should be alert and good looking. We are encouraged to look back to the cross and the tomb, while we are urged to look forward to the blessed hope. Unfortunately, people seem to be looking around at the world instead of focusing on Jesus.

Looking Around

Jesus reminds us that *"wisdom is justified by her children"* (Matthew 11:19). I have not been around much wisdom and my experience with the truth of that Scripture is limited. However, I have been able to witness the converse on far too many occasions. I can testify that stupidity will prove itself. Any theology that causes us to focus on the present evil world must be stupid. Why would anyone want to be bad looking? However, those who believe that the church is going to go through any part of the tribulation cannot be looking for Jesus. They are looking for the beast, they are looking for the false prophet, or they are looking at current events. They are bad looking.

We noticed that the annual competition of seasonal home beautification began earlier than usual this year. It started with one neighbor who placed a huge sleigh on his roof, replete with a larger than life size fat man in a red suit and all of the reindeer. Following his lead homes all over the neighborhood began to display decorated trees, manger scenes and lights, loads of lights, colored bulbs, flashing lights, strings of lights, each arrangement more spectacular than the other one before.

The homes were not the only place where the decorations emerged. In the malls and shopping places the signs began to pop up. Signs that warned about the limited number of shopping days left and the fat man in the red suit seemed to be everywhere. When you see these signs appearing in the community, you can be very certain that Thanksgiving is not far away.

I heard that little gag from a Bible teacher at Philadelphia Biblical University named Dr. Cawood. I am not that clever. However, I do love the lesson that it teaches. There are no signs for the holiday of Thanksgiving, but there are plenty of indications that Christmas is closing in on us. Dr. Cawood likened the relationship between Thanksgiving and the signs of Christmas that followed it, with the rapture and the indications that the tribulation, which follows it, may

Are We There Yet?

be upon us. There are no signs for the rapture. However like the Christmas season that follows Thanksgiving, there are signs for the great tribulation. As we look around we can see from the signs that the tribulation may be drawing near and that means that the blessed hope may not be far away.

When I was privileged to travel to Israel I spent my first night with friends who lived near Masada. They drove me through the desert to the backside of Masada and I toured the ancient site by myself late in the day. Not too long before, a Hollywood production crew made a movie depicting the historical events of Masada and left behind the engines of warfare. The equipment looked authentic to the times and I am certain that many a tourist has thought the apparatus to be of Roman manufacture and not Hollywood. That night I sent an e-mail home to my wife. I wanted her to know that I had arrived safely and I could not wait to tell her that I had stood in the very place where Peter O'Toole had stood.

In sending the e-mail I made a marvelous discovery. Using a Hebrew Typewriter I attempted to write "www". I never thought about it before, but there is no Hebrew letter "w". In order to write "w," I had to substitute the Hebrew letter ו vav. Now the neat thing about that is that the Hebrew language does not use the Arabic numerals, no surprise. Each Hebrew letter has a numerical value. א Aleph is one, ב Bet is two, ג Gimmel is three, ד Dalet is four, ה Heh is five and ו Vav is six. When I went to write "www," I wrote the Hebrew equivalent of 666!

> *"He causes all, both small and great, rich and poor, free and slave, to receive a mark in their right hand, or on their foreheads, and that no man may buy or sell except one who has the mark or the name of the beast, or the number of his name. Here is wisdom. Let him who has understanding calculate the number of the beast, for it is the number of a man: His number is 666."* Revelation 13:16-18

The book of Revelation speaks about the unusual mark of the beast. For two thousand years the prophecy made no sense and there seemed little reason or logical purpose for the economic mark. Today it all makes perfect sense largely because of two major issues in our society.

The first issue is substance abuse. Our world is plagued by the substance abuse dilemma even though we can stop drugs from entering our nation. We have the resources and we certainly have the technology. The problem is economics. We pay a guard $15.00 an hour to look for drugs and a drug dealer can pay him $200.00 to look the other way.

Meanwhile, an ever-increasing amount of the resources of our law enforcement agencies are exhausted in this war against drugs. At the same time addicts commit crimes to buy drugs. Our communities are no longer secure.

There seems to be an obvious solution. Remove cash from the society. Without cash there would be no motivation to sell drugs. The way our economy would work would be totally by computer. All paychecks would be directly deposited into our accounts and any purchases would be withdrawn automatically. All of us would carry a card that would identify us and we would use the card to conduct every transaction.

I realize that you could still barter for drugs. In fact the few drug users and dealers that I have had limited contact with in my life have taught me that there is a sub-economy that exists. They use drugs in lieu of cash. With drugs they can purchase a shirt or get a ride in a cab. Goods and services can be acquired by trading drugs.

But that only works because we have cash in the system. Eventually, the drugs or the stuff that they have been traded for have to be converted to dollars. How many television sets or VCR's or computers would a drug dealer want to accumulate? Without cash in our society valuables will have no value. This cashless solution could virtually eliminate robbery and greatly reduce crime.

Are We There Yet?

A second major issue in our society is the problem of security. In Israel they look for bombers, but in America our politically correct civilization forces us to try to look for bombs. Now instead of profiling, we search everyone.

I used to appreciate the freedom of travel that I enjoyed in America because I never needed to show my identification, or carry my cards with me. Those days are gone. National security issues could be addressed by forcing every citizen to carry a card. For security and identification purposes, every citizen could be assigned a web site. The card would contain economic information, which would access an individual's bank account as well as show identification. It would also contain the individual's web site information with the "www" address. There, a picture and description of the individual could be obtained. The idea of removing cash from our society and conducting all our business with cards and computers is ready for implementation.

The great difficulty with the ID/economic computer card is losing the card. I have a check/debit/credit card in my wallet. At least I think it is in my wallet. I have lost this card so many times that when I call the 800 customer service number to get the old card cancelled and to request a new card, they answer the phone by saying "Hello, Mitch."

We need to find a way to secure that card to the individual so that it could never be lost or stolen. The solution is obvious. We can take the information and we put it directly on the back of the hand of every citizen. This could be done in a very cosmetic way. The information would be invisible to the eye and only read by a computer scanner. That way we do not have to deal with pin numbers nor worry about having the card stolen or losing our card.

The only other difficulty that would arise is the amputee, a person with prosthetic hands. These folks could have the information placed on their foreheads. Everyone has a head, we just don't seem to use them.

We would no longer have to look for our cards every time we leave the house. We would not have to rummage through our purses and wallets. All the economic and identification information could be indelibly inscribed directly on our hands or on our foreheads. Only legal transactions would be recognized and money would be useless. All stores, merchants and services could be connected to the web. Each card could contain a "www" address and if Hebrew becomes the universal language then the mystery of 666 would be explained.

Our world is ready[7]. The mysterious "mark of the beast" now makes sense and the time for this concept has already arrived. In Revelation 14 we read how any person who receives the mark of the beast will suffer dire consequences. Well the exact words are *"he himself shall also drink of the wine of the wrath of God... He shall be tormented with fire and brimstone..."* (Revelation 14:10).

I am not certain what all that means, but it does not sound pleasant. The problem is that I have been promised eternal life but would probably receive the dreaded mark if I thought it could buy a pizza. Now, there is a way to keep us from the mark, which is to have us leave before the beast starts dishing out ID numbers.

In Revelation 11 we read about two witnesses. How *"their dead bodies will lie in the street of the great city... Then those from the peoples, tribes, tongues, and nations will see their dead bodies three-and-a-half days and not allow their dead bodies to be put into graves. And those who dwell on the earth will rejoice over them, make merry, and send gifts one to another, because these two prophets tormented those who dwell on the earth"* (Revelation 11:8-10).

The people of the earth, specifically different kinds of tongues and nations, will look at the two dead witnesses. This event could never have happened before a few short years ago. The introduction of television into our civilization has made this possible, but it still could not happen until the satellite communications systems were introduced.

Are We There Yet?

With satellite TV the whole world can watch the same event at the same time.

As we look around at our world, we see occurrences that make tribulation events possible and even plausible in the near future. As the tribulation draws near, we can be certain that the rapture is growing closer and as we look around, we see reasons why we should be looking up, for our redemption is drawing nigh.

CHAPTER TWO

One Taken, One Left

This title sounds like it could be the statistics after a base running blunder in a Phillies game. One was caught stealing and one left on base. Actually this phrase comes from Matthew 24:40-41 and there have been many blunders in regard to proper interpretation.

I have viewed films on prophecy that cite this verse and they show one person being taken and the other experiencing the Tribulation. I remember one scene where the husband disappeared and the wife finds his electric razor still buzzing, dangling from the chord. He was taken and she was left. The one left behind in the movie had to face the horrors of the one world ruler and all the perils of that time of unparalleled evil (Daniel 12:1).

That scene depicts a very popular understanding of the passage and it is a blunder. In Matthew 24:29 we read the phrase, *"Immediately after the tribulation of those days."* The events of Matthew 24:40-41 take place after the tribulation. The thinking is that if the people disappear after the tribulation then the rapture must take place at that time. It is true that people disappear at the end of the tribulation. Well, people are at least taken away at the end of the tribulation, but that is not the rapture. It is not the believers who are taken away, it is the unbelievers who are taken away.

Jesus explains this to us. He teaches us in Matthew 24:38 that His coming is like the days of Noah. Then He continues to explain how in the days of Noah *they* were eating, drinking, marrying and giving their daughters to marriage right up until the time that Noah entered the ark. In verse 39 Jesus says that *they* knew not until the flood came and took *them* all away.

The ones who are taken away by the flood are the unbelievers. The believers entered the ark and were carried over the tribulation from the troubles of the judgment on the world and were deposited back on the land to live out the rest of their lives. At the end of the Tribulation unbelievers are taken away in judgment and the believers enter Christ's kingdom on earth.

Apparently, despite the horrors of the great tribulation, many people will continue to live as if there were no impending doom or coming judgment. Such is the nature of man. We eat, we drink, we go on with our lives and we ignore the ultimate judgment of God.

I was speaking with a man who sells vacation plans for a living. He travels extensively and makes elaborate preparations for every trip he takes. I asked him about his final journey. He was not prepared. He knows that it is appointed unto every man to die (Hebrew 9:27). He may not have read the Scriptures, but all anyone has to do is stay alive and after a while, you will learn that we have to face the reality of a final journey.

I imagine that toll collectors on the turnpike find it fascinating that people can drive for hundreds of miles and when they get to the tollbooth they seem surprised and unprepared to pay the toll. What did you think would happen at the tollbooth? How can you drive all that distance and not be prepared for the toll?

I asked my salesmen friend, "How can you live your entire life making travel plans and not make provisions for the inevitable final journey?"

It sounds crazy and it is crazy, but it is the nature of man. It is like the proverbial ostrich, which sees a lion and then buries its head in the sand. The ostrich is not trying to hide from the lion, but is only covering its eyes and holding its nose so it cannot see or smell the lion. We do not want to sense in any way the coming bad news. This is why man has always killed the prophets and stoned those that were sent by God to warn them. It is why Christians suffer persecution; because our generation wants to eat, drink, marry and give in marriage without a sniff of the impending doom. They do not want to pay the toll taker at the end of the ride.

Jesus speaks about this aspect of human nature in Matthew 24:37-42 when he warns about the judgment at the end of the tribulation. This judgment is mentioned in the parable of the wheat and the tares, which is explained for us in Matthew 13:38-43. Jesus teaches us further about this judgment in the parable of the dragnet in Matthew 13:47-50.[1] In both parables and in the Olivet discourse of Matthew 24, Jesus teaches us that at the end of the tribulation, at the end of the world as we know it, all the unbelievers will be taken away in judgment.

In Matthew 25, Jesus begins to describe that judgment scene as the servants who were given talents being judged by works. The standard was what did they do with the talents entrusted to their care? To the believer God says, *"Well done, good and faithful servant...enter into the joy of your lord."* Concerning the unbeliever, we read in Matthew 25:30, *"cast the unprofitable servant into the outer darkness."*

The basis for judgment is works, but the basis for salvation is faith. This concept is repeated in the next parable with the sheep and the goats. The faithful expressed their faith with how well they cared for the brethren of Jesus.[2] To the unbeliever Jesus says, *"Depart from Me, you cursed, into the everlasting fire prepared for the devil and his angels."* Or, as we read in Matthew 24, the unbeliever is taken away.

Are We There Yet?

Those who believe in the post tribulation rapture[3], do so because they misunderstand Matthew 24:39. When you realize that the person being removed is the unbeliever, you remove all Biblical basis for the post tribulation rapture view.

Around twenty years ago I was privileged to speak in a large church each summer. Their pastor went to a conference and in his absence I was given the opportunity to preach. They requested that I speak on eschatology, so each year I conducted a mini prophecy conference.

One very unusual procedure of this church was that the Adult Sunday School class would take up an offering for Jewish missions every week and it was placed in an interest-bearing account throughout the year. When I came to speak in the summer, the church would give me the entire amount as an honorarium. Usually the honorariums were several thousand dollars. I never kept the honorariums as it went directly to the mission, as it should. However, whenever anyone collected an honorarium of that size people noticed. I usually received honorariums between fifty and one hundred and fifty dollars. When I came in with a multi thousand-dollar check, I could interrupt staff meetings, speak out of turn and present dissenting opinions and everyone kept smiling at me.

One year the pastor asked me if I could bring a message from the post-tribulation position. He did not expect me to teach against my beliefs, nor did he require me to change my theology. His request was really quite reasonable. All the pastor wanted me to do was to present to the congregation the Scriptures that support that position. He asked me to teach the belief and the reasons why some might hold to it. I told him that I would have to do some research and then I would get back to him.

I forget all the books and commentaries that I read. I do recall that I tried to discover any and all support for the position. The more I studied, the more I became convinced that there was no Scriptural support for the belief that the Church will go through any part of the Tribulation.

I phoned the pastor and related to him my findings and he was truly disappointed. He expressed his gratitude to me and then called another Jewish missionary to replace me that year and every year since.

The conclusion is rather simple. If one shred of evidence existed for the post-tribulation position, I would never have turned down the honorariums of that magnitude. That should convince everyone that knows me.

Message from the Weeks

I have a theory. My theory is that people, who love math, are not people who love people. According to my theory people who love people usually teach subjects like English and history.

The math teachers tend to be a sterner lot. They love their subject, but they scare the little kids. Many of us grow up afraid of numbers. My theory explains why, when the bill at a fast food restaurant comes to $5.17 and you hand the clerk a ten dollar bill and 17 cents, he glares at you like you committed a crime. The calculation of exact change is overwhelmingly complicated. The blank stares and furrowed brows would make you think they were trying to ascertain the reentry trajectory for a lunar module.

My theory also explains why when we come to the prophecy of Daniel 9:24-27 many Christians freeze up like a deer in the headlights. It involves math. I understand that your math teacher was a real meanie. I am certain he was scary and now we all hate to do arithmetic. Please try to relax. Before your ears start to bleed, we can attempt to study the passage slowly and simply.

> *"Seventy weeks are determined for your people and for your holy city, to finish the transgression, to make an end of sins, to make*

reconciliation for iniquity, to bring in everlasting righteousness, to seal up the vision and prophecy, and to anoint the Most Holy Know therefore and understand, that from the going forth of the commandment to restore and to build Jerusalem until Messiah the Prince, there shall be seven weeks and sixty- two weeks; the street shall be built again, and the wall, even in troublesome times. And after the sixty-two weeks Messiah shall be cut off, but not for Himself; and the people of the prince who is to come shall destroy the city and the sanctuary. The end of it shall be with a flood, and till the end of the war desolations are determined. Then he shall confirm a covenant with many for one week; but in the middle of the week he shall bring an end to sacrifice and offering. And on the wing of abominations shall be one who makes desolate, even until the consummation which is determined, is poured out on the desolate". Daniel 9:24-27

This prophecy is given to Daniel towards the end of the Babylonian captivity.[4] It is given to Daniel in three different sections; each section refers to a different period of time, but each section deals with the Jewish people. The expression *"your people"* (Daniel 9:24, 10:14, 11:14), the city of Jerusalem (Daniel 9:16, 24), the Jewish Messiah, the Jewish liturgical system and the Jewish scriptures all assure us that the passage is referring to the Jewish people. This prophecy is concerned not with world history or church history, but with the history of Israel and the city of Jerusalem.

The prophecy does not mention the church as there are no references to apostles, epistles, elders, deacons, baptism, communion, Sunday School or Sunday services. The prophecy is specifically declared to be about the people of Daniel. This prophecy is given to the Jews. Remember, in the church there are neither Jews nor Gentiles but all are one (Galatians 3:28, Colossians 3:11).

The total prophecy spans a period of seventy weeks. In our language a week is a collection of seven days. In the biblical language the word week refers to a collection of seven years. Whereas people today think in units of tens (decades), Daniel's people thought in terms of sevens (heptads). Seven days are in one week. Every seventh year was a Sabbath rest year (Lev. 25:1-7). Seven "sevens" brought them to the Year of Jubilee (Lev. 25:8-12). Seventy "sevens," then, is a span of 490 years. The Lord promised to accomplish six things for Israel within the time frame of these 490 years.

> God will *finish the transgression of* Israel.
> God will *put an end to sin.*
> God will *make atonement for iniquity.*
> God will *bring in eternal righteousness.*
> God will *seal up the vision and prophecy.*
> God will *anoint the most holy.*

The starting point of the prophecy is the decree to return, rebuild and restore the city of Jerusalem. The rebuilding of the wall in times of trouble is mentioned in the prophecy. There are four different times when decrees were made and the Jewish people were allowed to return from Babylon.[5] This reference to the wall identifies the decree as the one recorded in Nehemiah 2, which occurs in 445 B.C. and gives us the starting date for the prophecy.

There are three distinct sections in this prophecy. The total length of time that is to elapse is the 70, seven-year periods. The first section is to last 7 weeks or, in our terminology, 49 years. The second section is described as 62 sevens, that is to say 62 weeks or 434 years. The first two sections combine to total 69 weeks or 483 years Since the entire prophecy entails a total of 70 weeks, or 490 years, there are 7 years, or one week that is left and that week would constitute the length of the third section.

The first section of the prophecy takes place from 445 B.C. until approximately the year 396 B.C.[6] In 396 B.C. the Old Testament canon[7] was completed and sealed up. From that completion we begin the second section of the prophecy. The 62 sevens (434 years) extend up to the triumphal entry of Messiah Jesus into the city of Jerusalem[8] on March 30, in the year 33 A.D., just prior to the time when the anointed One was *cut off*. The third section of the prophecy is the remaining week, a period of seven lunar years or a total of 2520 days. This last section is the great tribulation. It does not follow the other two sections immediately.

First, Daniel mentions two other events. In Daniel 9:26 we read *"And after the sixty-two weeks Messiah shall be cut off, but not for Himself."* After the second section of the prophecy has run its course, the Messiah will be cut off. Jesus entered the city of Jerusalem on Palm Sunday at the exact day that Daniel had predicted about 500 years earlier. On Friday of that week Jesus was sacrificed on the cross at Calvary.

Daniel 9:26 continues to say, *"and the people of the prince who is to come shall destroy the city and the sanctuary."* Three facts are mentioned here. First the city and the sanctuary are to be destroyed. This occurred in the year 70 A.D. the second fact is that there is a prince who is coming. The third fact is that the prince is going to come from the same people who destroy the city and the sanctuary. The people who destroyed the city and the sanctuary were the Romans so the end time ruling prince that shall come must be Roman.

Daniel 9:26 concludes with *"The end of it shall be with a flood, and till the end of the war desolations are determined."* The last week, the seventieth week, the last seven-year period that deals with the nation of Israel will end with a flood.

We can read about the tribulation in Revelation 12:15-16, *"So the serpent spewed water out of his mouth like a flood after the woman, that he might cause her to be carried away by the flood. But the earth helped the woman, and the earth opened its mouth and swallowed up the flood which the dragon had spewed out of his mouth."* In Matthew 24 Jesus speaks about people on the rooftops of their homes. In thirty years of meeting and ministering to Jewish people I have known exactly one Jewish roofer. The warnings of Matthew 24 are not written to the Jewish roofers of the tribulation. Rather, Jesus is speaking about the flood when everyone has climbed out on the roof to escape the rising water.

In Daniel 9:26 we see how the third section of the prophecy is to end. In verse 27 we are told how the great tribulation begins. Daniel 9:27 reads, *"Then he shall confirm a covenant with many for one week."* When Israel confirms an existing peace treaty with the end time Roman ruler, the seven-year tribulation begins officially.

In Biblical times contracts were written on scrolls. The cutting of the scroll signified the cutting of the contract. An interesting "play on words" occurs here in the Hebrew. In the phrase "the Messiah is cut off" the word translated "cut off" is the same word used when a contract is cut. The Jewish people violently cut off their Messiah then they cut a contract with the false Messiah. Jesus said, *"I have come in my Father's name, and you do not receive me; if another comes in his own name, him you will receive."* (John 5:43)

Recently I needed to run an errand and I could not find the car keys. When I finally found them, I forgot where I wanted to go. We have spent so much time looking for the keys in Daniel 9 that we may have forgotten where it was we initially wanted to go.

The book of Daniel records an amazingly accurate prophecy regarding the nation of Israel. That prophecy was given in three segments. The first phase of the prophecy began in 445 B.C. and ended in 396 B.C. During that timeframe there was no church. The second phase of the prophecy begins in 396 B.C. and concludes in 33 A.D. when Jesus entered Jerusalem. Again the church had not yet been formed. In Matthew 16, Jesus was speaking to Peter about the great confession that Peter had just made in regard to the true nature of the Lord. In verse 18 we read *"upon this rock I will build my church"*. The church is yet future to the ministry of the Lord Jesus. In Acts 11:15 Peter refers back to the day of Pentecost and calls it *"the beginning."* The church begins after the 69th week of Daniel's prophecy.

All seventy weeks of Daniel's prophecy pertain to the nation of Israel. The church is not in the first 69 weeks and the church will not be in the 70th week either. The 70th week of Daniel does not immediately follow the 69th week. The 69th week ended with the Lord entering Jerusalem in the year 33. The people, of the prince that shall come destroyed the city of Jerusalem in the year 70. The final week of Daniel's prophecy had yet to begin.

There is a gap between the 69th and the 70th week. The church age begins within that gap. The church began with the supernatural invasion of the Holy Spirit into the time-space universe at the Jewish holiday of Pentecost. The church age will end with the supernatural translation of the church as the Holy Spirit is taken away at the rapture. The entire church age exists within the gap between the weeks. The 70 weeks of Daniel belong to Israel. The church does not exist in any of those weeks, including the 70th week, which is the time of Jacob's trouble, the Great Tribulation.

Message From The Feasts

In Leviticus 23, God records the seven Levitical holidays. Then in Colossians 2:16–17 we read, *"Let no man judge you in food or in drink, or regarding a festival or a new moon or Sabbaths, which are a shadow of things to come, but the body is of Christ."* These two verses draw a beautiful picture for us. In eternity future, we see a light that shines on events in time. The shining light on these events casts a shadow. When a body casts a shadow on the ground, we often recognize the body from the shadow. The Levitical feasts are the shadow and the body is the Messiah, or rather the events in time in the ministry in the life of the Messiah. The feasts of Israel are darkened representatives of the actual events in time. As we study the feasts we can learn about the advents of the Lord.

There are seven *feasts of the Lord* not counting the Sabbath given to the Jewish people in Leviticus 23. The weekly Sabbath, which teaches us to cease from our own labors, as God did from His, is not referenced in Colossians. It would be called "the Sabbath" and Colossians refers to a multiple of sabbath Days. The seven Levitical feasts pre-picture some aspect of the life and ministry of the Lord.

The first of these feasts is the Passover,[9] which is supposed to begin on the 14th day of the Hebrew month of Nisan. On that day the Jewish people were instructed to bring a lamb into their homes[10]. The lamb was to come from either the sheep or the goats. It had to be a male in the prime of its life. The lamb was then examined to be certain it was without blemish and without spot. On the afternoon of the fourteenth of Nisan the lamb was to be slain *in the evening* (Exodus 12:6), literally in the Hebrew (*between the evenings*), which is three in the afternoon.[11] The blood of the lamb was to be applied to the two side posts of the door and the upper doorpost of the house. Those instructions resulted in each Jewish home drawing a bloody cross on their door. Every Jewish home that was protected by the bloody cross would be spared, but every home without a cross would experience the death of the firstborn, which in some cases would be their only begotten sons.

Fourteen hundred years after that first Passover Jesus, the only begotten son of God, died on a bloody cross. The Passover was a shadow of the cross of Calvary. Jesus is called *our Passover* in 1 Corinthians 5:7; Jesus is called the *"Lamb of God"* in John 1:29 and 1:36. In 1 Peter 1:19 Jesus is likened to *"a lamb without blemish and without spot,"* a direct reference to the Passover lamb. In Revelation 5:6-13 we see Jesus as the worthy lamb that was slain. Revelation refers to Jesus as the lamb in an additional eleven places (6:16; 7:9-17; 12:11; 13:8; 14:1-10; 15:3; 17:14; 19:7-9; 21:14; 22-23; 22:1-3).

The Passover lamb was to be roasted with fire and then entirely consumed in one night. Nothing pertaining to the lamb was permitted to remain in the house. The lamb had to be totally consumed before the feast of unleavened bread, which began on the following day. Unusually, the Scriptures also admonished the Jewish people that not a bone of the lamb was to be broken. The Hebrew Scriptures reference the unbroken bones four different times (Exodus 12:46, Numbers 9:12, Psalm 22:17, 34:20).

The Roman method of capitol punishment was crucifixion. We are all aware of the fact that crucifixion is an excruciating way to die. Some of us knew that without spending $8 and 3 hours at the movies. People who are being crucified need to push themselves up with their legs to breathe. Breaking their legs would prohibit them from breathing and they would expire within minutes. In John's Gospel (John 19:3-36) we read how the Jewish leaders wanted to be certain that the men on the cross would be removed before sundown because the following day was the first day of the feast of unleavened bread and as such was a special Sabbath day.[12] They besought Pilate to get permission to break the legs of the men who were being crucified. When they came to Jesus, they discovered that He was no longer alive and there was no need to break His legs. John writes that this was done that the Scriptures might be fulfilled which said, that not a bone of the Old Testament lamb was to be broken.

The Old Testament lamb had been slain, roasted and devoured, yet the Scriptures forbade the Jewish people from breaking a single one of the lamb's bones. The command certainly was not given to protect the lamb that was already slain. The command was given so that the Old Testament lamb would be the perfect example of the Lord Jesus.

The Roman soldiers did not kill Jesus and He did not die from them breaking His legs. Jesus did not die from being crucified. Jesus said, *"Father, into Your hands I commit My spirit." Having said this, He breathed His last."*(Luke 23:46) Jesus dismissed His life with dignity, nobility and majesty. Nobody killed Jesus. Nobody could kill Jesus. Jesus is God and He willingly sacrificed Himself, in love, for our benefit. The threefold admonishment not to break a bone of the Old Testament lamb forces us to focus on the fact that Jesus died willingly. The Passover lamb is a type of the Lamb of God and the holiday of Passover is a clear picture of the Lord Jesus.

The second holiday is the Feast of Unleavened Bread. According to the Scriptures the feast begins on the 15th of Nisan.[13] Today the Jewish people celebrate Passover on the 15th. The night of the exodus from Egypt the Jewish people could not wait for their bread to rise so, to remember that event, they are instructed to abstain from leaven for the entire week.

We recognize that leaven is a symbol of sin (Matthew 13:33, 16:6, 1 Corinthians 5:6, Galatians 5:6-9). Unleavened bread is a picture of something or someone sinless. Most Jewish homes conduct a special meal in their homes on the 15th of Nisan, a Passover Seder.[14] On the Seder table there are three pieces of unleavened bread, matzo, placed together on a tray, an Echad holder or unity container. Before dinner the leader of the service is instructed to reach into the container and remove the middle piece of matzo. He breaks the middle matzo and leaves one half between the two whole slices. The other half is wrapped in a white linen napkin and hidden away until the end of the service.

The reason the rabbis give for breaking the matzo is to enable us to recite a prayer called, "this is the bread of distress." Since people in distress make their meals with broken pieces rather than whole slices, they break the matzo. I once asked a rabbi, "Why do we recite the prayer 'This Is the Bread of Distress'?" The answer was predictable as he told me that we recite the prayer because we just broke the matzo. I love it. According to the rabbis, we break the matzo to recite the prayer and we recite the prayer because we just broke the matzo. I do not think they have all the information.

At the end of the meal, the half matzo that was hidden is now searched for. It is called the aphikomen. The child who finds the hidden matzo is given a reward. The leader of the service then takes the matzo and breaks it into olive size pieces. The matzo is then distributed to everyone at the table. This piece of matzo represents the meat of the Passover offering. It is the last thing to be eaten. It is the dessert of the meal so that its taste will remain uppermost in the mouth.

Jesus was celebrating Passover the night that he instituted communion. He took the aphikomen and said, *"this is My body"* (Matthew 26:26, Mark 14:22, Luke 22:19, 1 Corinthians 11:24). The aphikomen is a picture of the body of the Lord Jesus. Matzo is striped and pierced. Jesus is the striped and pierced One. Psalm 22:16 reads, *"They pierced My hands and feet."* In Zechariah 12:10 we read, *"then they will look on Me whom they pierced. Yes, they will mourn for Him as one mourns for his only son."* This passage is marvelous. God is speaking and He is both pierced and He is the son, clearly depicting the deity of Jesus.

In Isaiah 53 we read how Jesus is pierced through for our transgressions and how we are healed by His stripes (Isaiah 53:5). The unleavened bread is sinless and perfect, broken and buried and raised up. The unleavened bread is the second part of a three-part unity.[15]

Some haggadas[16] refer to the Echad as a picture of the Patriarchs. The three pieces of matzo represent Abraham, Isaac and Jacob. Other haggadas see the God of Abraham, the God of Isaac and the God of Jacob in the three pieces of matzo. The three pieces of matzo are a unity, which I think picture the unity of God. I think the picture is God the Father, God the Son and God the Holy Spirit. The middle piece, which pictures God the Son, is broken out of the unity container. Half remains between the two whole slices to show that He is 100% God. The other half shows that He is also 100% man. As a man He is broken, is buried and then raised on the third cup to show a third day resurrection.[17]

The Feast of Unleavened Bread begins on the 15th of Nisan and continues for seven days. Within those seven days there will be a Saturday Sabbath. The day following the Saturday Sabbath in that week is the holiday of First Fruits (Leviticus 23:11). The Chumash,[18] in comment on Leviticus 23:11 writes, *"Although the word שבת ordinarily refers to the Sabbath, this cannot be the case here, because the verse does not specify which of the fifty-two Sabbaths is meant (Rashi; Sifra). This term becomes one of the major points of controversy between the Sages and the heretical Boethusians. They interpret the term literally, as referring to the Sabbath, thus claiming that the Omer had to be brought on a Sunday, the morrow of the Sabbath (Menachos 65a)."*

According to the Chumash, a controversy exists. Can you imagine? Rabbis arguing over a point of doctrine? I'm shocked! Actually, I am a bit surprised to see that the majority of the traditional Jewish expositors refuse to interpret the passage in a simple, literal manner. They insist that the Sabbath in question cannot be a weekly Sabbath since the text did not specify which of the fifty-two Sabbaths was meant. A specific Shabbat has to be in view because they are told to count seven Saturdays from that starting date. However, the text does identify which specific Sabbath is in view. The week of the celebration of Unleavened Bread was just explained.

Unleavened Bread is a seven-day celebration, which began on the 15th of Nisan. The first day, the 15th of Nisan, is a Sabbath day. The last day, which would fall on the 21st of Nisan, would also be a Sabbath day. If either of these Sabbaths were the specific Sabbath in view the Scriptures could easily identify them by date. We could easily read "start counting on the 22nd of Nisan" or "start counting on the 16th of Nisan". Instead, we're told to start counting on the day after the Sabbath. It is obvious that we cannot know the date; the number of the day within the month of the Sabbath. Therefore it must be the weekly Sabbath that occurs within the week of the Feast of Unleavened Bread.

Whatever day the feast begins on, there will always be one Saturday somewhere within the week. There are only seven days in a week. And a seven-day-long celebration will include every one of the days of the week. It is like magic how that works. The day following that Sabbath, will be a Sunday. The morrow following a Saturday is always a Sunday. Even in a lunar calendar Sunday follows Saturday. Even in a religious Jewish calendar Sunday follows Saturday. That Sunday was the Feast of First Fruits.

The Sunday after the Sabbath of the week in which Jesus entered Jerusalem was arguably the most significant day in the history of mankind. On that day Jesus rose from the dead. The Old Testament holiday called for bringing an "Omar," a measure of ground barley from the first harvest to the priest. The priest waves the offering before the Lord *"to be accepted"*(Leviticus 23:11). The Chumash translates the phrase *to gain favor for you.* The offering gains favor or acceptability before the Lord for the person who is bringing the offering. The word translated *"to be accepted"* is the Hebrew word רָצוֹן "ratson". According to the "Theological Wordbook of the Old Testament", that word *"frequently describes God's pleasure with his servants, particularly referred to the Messiah."*(Isaiah 42:1) In Micah 6:7, "ratson" is used to express the satisfaction of a debt; specifically the atonement for sin.

Jesus, the Messiah, the one who makes atonement for sin, is raised from the dead as the first fruits of them that sleep (1 Corinthians 15:20). He was raised on the day that the priest was supposed to wave an offering before the Lord to gain our acceptance. Instead, *Jesus* gains our acceptance before the Lord and the empty tomb is the proof that the debt has been paid. The first three feasts picture the Lord Jesus, Passover, the Feast of Unleavened Bread and the Feast of First Fruits.

The fourth feast is called Shavuos, the Hebrew word for weeks. The controversy over when the holiday of First Fruits occurs carries over to the day of Shavuos. Beginning on the holiday of First Fruits, the Jewish people are instructed to count seven Sabbaths and then on the day following the seventh Sabbath they are to celebrate the holiday of Shavuos. The Chumash reads, *"Unlike all the other festivals Shavuos is not identified as a specific day in the Jewish calendar."*

Actually if Shavuos were fifty days after the 15th of Nisan as the rabbis believe, then it *would* occur on a specific day in the Jewish calendar. It would always occur on the 6th of Sivan. Since it actually takes place fifty days after the weekly Sabbath that occurs during the week of Unleavened Bread, then it will always be on a different calendar date, but it will always fall on the same day of the week. Every Saturday is followed by a Sunday and the day after the seventh Sabbath will still be Sunday. The day of the resurrection is the day that they begin counting. From that day seven Sabbaths shall be complete and the morrow following the seventh Sabbath, the fiftieth day, that Sunday is the day of Shavuos (Leviticus 23:15-16), or as it is named in the New Testament, the day of Pentecost (Acts 2:1).

Regardless of when one thinks the counting of fifty days should begin, the day of Shavuos coincides with the day of Pentecost. On that holiday two wave offerings are brought together as first fruits before the Lord. Seven lambs are brought first. The number seven is often the number of completion, showing the completion of the sacrifice system. Next, two rams are brought as one offering with one young bullock. The two wave offerings and the two rams brought as one, show the unity of the body of Christ.

In the body of Christ both Jew and Gentile are united as one. In Ephesians 2:14-15 we read " *For He Himself is our peace, who has made both one, and has broken down the middle wall of separation,[19] having abolished in His flesh the enmity, that is, the law of commandments contained in ordinances, so as to create in Himself one new man from the two, thus making peace.*" In 1 Corinthians 12:13 we read, "*For by one Spirit we were all baptized into one body em whether Jews or Greeks...*" The Spirit descends on the day of Pentecost and on this Jewish holiday the Church, the body of Christ, is born. For fourteen hundred years Israel celebrated the birthday of the Church and we do not even send the Jewish people a card.

The Jewish people are instructed to count the days from Passover to Shavuos. The counting "recalls the days in the wilderness immediately after the Exodus when the Jewish people excitedly counted the days, each day improving and elevating themselves, so that they would be worthy of receiving the Torah."[20]

"According to Rabbinic interpretation of the Bible (B. Shab. 86b-88a)," the day that Moses was given the law at Mt. Sinai was the 6th of Sivan. Shavuos commemorates this event when it emphasizes the sanctity of the Torah.[21]

In Jeremiah 31 we read about the New Covenant and its contrast with the contract that was given at Mt. Sinai. The law that was given at Sinai is replaced by the indwelling of the Spirit (Jeremiah 31:33). The day of Pentecost, which is the holiday of Shavuos, commemorates the giving of the law and it is the day that the Holy Spirit descended upon the disciples. In Romans we read how the law of the Spirit of life has made us free from the law of sin and death (Romans 8:2). *"The fruit of the Spirit is love, joy, peace, longsuffering, kindness, goodness, faithfulness, gentleness, self-control. Against such there is no law."* Galatians 5:22-23

The comparison between the law and the Spirit is clearly seen in John's gospel where the Lord promises to send the Comforter. We see that the Spirit of truth will abide with us forever (John 14:16-17). The law and the Spirit both last forever (Matthew 5:18). They are both truth (John 17:17). Also, just as the law was given exclusively to Israel, so the world cannot receive the Spirit.

In John 14:26, we see that the Spirit will teach us all things. The law previously was our schoolmaster (Galatians 3:24) now it is the Spirit. Jesus says that the Law of Moses spoke about Him in John 5:39. In Luke 24:27 the Lord explained all that the law taught in regards to Him. In John 15:26 we see that it would be the Spirit who was soon to come who would testify of Jesus. In John 16:8 we read how the coming Spirit would convict the world of sin, righteousness and judgment. In Romans 7:7-13 we see that conviction of sin was formerly the role of the law. Each of the first four Levitical holidays depicts an aspect of the first advent of the Lord. Passover points to the unblemished lamb and Unleavened Bread pictures His body, first fruits and the resurrection. Shavuos is Pentecost, the birthday of the Church, the body of Christ. Leviticus 23 begins with the often used Hebrew phrase, וידבר יהוה אל־מֹשֶׁה לֵּאמֹר: דבר אל־בני יִשְׂרָאֵל. This phrase is translated, *"And the Lord spoke to Moses saying, "Speak to the children of Israel."* This phrase introduces the discussion of the feasts. Leviticus 23:1-3 deals with the weekly Sabbath. After the Sabbath the seven Levitical feasts are introduced in verses 4-22.

Leviticus 23:4-5	Passover	Christ our Passover
Leviticus 23:6-8	Unleavened Bread	His Body
Leviticus 23:9-14	First Fruits	Resurrection
Leviticus 23:15-21	Shavuos	Pentecost

After 21 verses dealing with the feasts days, a new subject is suddenly introduced.

> *"When you reap the harvest of your land, thou shall not wholly reap the corners of your field when thou reap, nor shall you gather any gleaning from your harvest. You shall leave them for the poor and for the stranger: I am the Lord your God."* Leviticus 23:22

Leviticus 23:22 seems to be out of place in a discussion of feast days. There are two similar verses in the Torah.

> *"When you reap the harvest of your land, you shall not wholly reap the corners of your field, nor shall you gather the gleanings of your harvest."* Leviticus 19:9

The following verses give further and fuller exhortation.

> *"And you shall not glean your vineyard, nor shall you gather every grape of your vineyard; you shall leave them for the poor and the stranger: I am the Lord your God."* Leviticus 19:10

> *"When you reap your harvest in your field, and forget a sheaf in the field, you shall not go back to get it; it shall be for the stranger, the fatherless, and the widow, that the Lord thy God may bless you in all the work of your hands. When thou beat your olive trees, you shall not go over the boughs again; it shall be for the stranger, the fatherless, and the widow. When you gather the grapes of your vineyard, you shall not glean it afterward; it shall be for the stranger, the fatherless, and the widow"* Deuteronomy 24:19-21.

None of the passages use the imperative mood.[22] The sense of a command comes from the context. The context of Leviticus 23:22 is very different from the other two passages. Both in the Deuteronomy passage and in Leviticus 19 there is reference to the fields and vineyards.

In Leviticus 23, only the field is mentioned. Leviticus 23:22 reads differently from the other passages dealing with leaving the gleanings for the poor; in fact, it reads differently from the rest of the entire chapter, which deals with the feasts. Leviticus 23:22 could be read as a future tense, indicative mood.[23] There might not be any command expressed.

Rather, the verse just might be a prophetic one. I think the field is metaphysical. In John 4:35 Jesus speaks about the field that is white for harvest. In John 4:38 Jesus tells the disciples that He is sending them to reap where they have not sown; they are finishing the job that others have started. In Matthew 9:37-38 Jesus tells His disciples how the harvest is plenteous, but the laborers are few. In Matthew 13:38 Jesus explains the parable of the tares of the field. He tells the disciples that the field is the world. Israel has sown seed into the world and Leviticus says that the poor and the stranger will finish the reaping. In Ephesians 2:12, the Scriptures, in writing to the church say, *"you were... aliens from the commonwealth of Israel and strangers from the covenants of promise, having no hope and without God in the world."* The poor and the stranger are the spiritually bankrupt Gentiles who will, after Pentecost, combine with believing Jewish people and form the Church.

Leviticus 23:22 is a gap that interrupts the discussion of Israel's feasts. The first four feasts coincide with the early rains that fall in the land of Israel. Following the early rains there is a long hot dry summer. At the conclusion of the summer the three fall feasts of Israel occur. The three fall feasts coincide with the latter rains.

There is a gap between the discussion of the feasts. There is a gap between the 69th and the 70th week of Daniel's prophecy. There is gap between the rainy seasons, the Church exists in the gap. Scriptures connect the two rainy seasons with the two aspects of the appearance of the Lord.

"He will come to us as the rain, like the rain, like the latter and former rain to the earth"(Hosea 6:3). James urges us to be patient in waiting for the coming of the Lord and likens our patience to the farmer waiting to receive both the early and then the latter rain (James 5:7).

After the summer has passed the first fall feast is celebrated. After the gap of Leviticus 23:22 the discussion of the feasts continues. In verse 23 we are instructed to observe a memorial of blowing of trumpets on the first day of the month of Tishri. The Rabbis call this day Rosh Hashanah, which literally means "the head of the year". According to tradition, on Rosh Hashanah, all the inhabitants of the world pass before the Lord in judgment like a flock of sheep. All are judged on Rosh Hashanah and the verdict is sealed on Yom Kippur.[24]

The discussion of Rosh Hashanah continues for 23 pages in the "Guide to Jewish Religious Practices and Customs". The Rabbis consume twenty three pages discussing the blowing of the shofar, the Scripture reading, the appropriate prayers, the various religious services and the traditional practices that are to be observed on Rosh Hashanah. The Torah mentions the day in three different passages. It is first mentioned here in Leviticus 23:23-25 and it is further referenced in two locations in the book of Numbers (10:10 and 29:1-6). A topic that the Bible exhausts in 9 sentences or verses takes the tradition 23 pages of elaboration.

In the 9 verses in the Bible we will read nothing about Judgment Day, about a New Year, or about casting bread upon the waters. The Bible instruction in Leviticus is rather simple. *"In the seventh month on the first day of the month, you shall have a Sabbath-rest, a memorial of blowing of trumpets, a holy convocation. You shall do no customary work on it; and you shall offer an offering made by fire, to the Lord."* Leviticus 23:24-25

The day is declared to be a Sabbath day, which should be easy enough to understand; a day of rest. I like that, I am a lazy kind of guy. The second thing we learn is that it is a memorial day, a day of sounding of trumpets. We are not told exactly what we are to remember, but we are told that we use the trumpets to call our attention to the memorial. The third aspect mentioned in Leviticus is, there is a sacrifice that is to be made by fire unto the Lord.

In Numbers we are told that the sacrifice is in addition to the daily sacrifice and that the sacrifice is to be comprised of *"one young bull, one ram and seven lambs in their first year, without blemish"*(Numbers 29:2). In addition, we are to offer one kid of the goats as a sin offering to make atonement.[25] And of course no sacrifice would be complete without the meat offering of flour mingled with oil, three tenth deals for the bullock, two tenth deals for the ram and one tenth deal for one lamb.

It is impossible to observe the sacrifice today. There is only one location where a sacrifice was to be offered and that was on the altar, in the Temple, in Jerusalem. The Temple is in ruins and Jewish people are hardly even allowed on the Temple Mount, which lies under Arab jurisdiction.

Even if I could find a place to bring my offering, I still could not observe the sacrifice. In the town where I live we are not permitted any open fires. Where I live there are laws prohibiting us from slaughtering animals.

The feasts of Israel were given to Israel. The Jewish people were to practice the feasts in the shadow of the Temple. The feasts themselves were a shadow of things to come. Jesus coming to the earth is the fullness that casts the shadow.

The chief characteristic of the Rosh Hashanah service is the blowing of the trumpets. In Numbers 10 we see the various functions that the trumpets played in the life of the nation of Israel. They were instructed to fashion two silver trumpets, which were to be used for calling assemblies, for war, for journeying and for making camps. When one trump was sounded, the princes of Israel gathered. When the second trumpet was sounded, which would be the last trump, the entire congregation of Israel was to gather at the door of the outer court.

> In 1 Corinthians 15:51-52 we read, *"Behold, I show you a mystery: We shall not all sleep, but we shall all be changed em in a moment, in the twinkling of an eye, at the last trumpet. For the trumpet will sound, and the dead will be raised incorruptible, and we shall be changed."*

The first time I read that verse was on the nursery room wall at Calvary Baptist Church. At first glance I thought the verse was speaking about diapers and naps. Now I realize that the sleepers are those believers who have died in Jesus.

There are only two kinds of believers, those who are alive and those who are dead. It might be difficult to tell them apart. I suppose the major difference is the truly dead believers do not complain as much as those who are alive. One day the dead will be raised and changed and the living will not have to be raised but will also need to be changed. Corruption must put on incorruption because this mortal body is not designed for heaven, so this mortal body needs to be translated.

The passage mentions that this change, this translation of the mortal body, takes place at the time of the last trump. The Scripture repeats emphatically *"for the trumpet will sound"*. In 1 Thessalonians 4:16 we read about this translation again, and again we are introduced to the trumpet. *"The Lord Himself will descend from heaven with a shout, with the voice of the archangel and with the trumpet of God"*.

When the trumpet would be sounded the entire congregation of Israel would be called to assemble at the door of the outer court. The outer court was the area of the Temple where the Gentiles were permitted. The Church consists of Jews and Gentiles who are made one in faith. The majestic gathering of the unified Church casts a shadow. That shadow is the trumpet blast of the feast of Rosh Hashanah.

Remember, the first four feasts look to the first appearance of Messiah Jesus. There is a gap between the spring feasts and the fall feasts. In that gap in Leviticus 23, the Church age is cryptically referred to in the gleaning of the field. At the sound of the trumpet the Church is gathered together to be with the Lord and sometime after that the 70th week of Daniel, the time of Israel's tribulation begins.

Following the Rosh Hashanah instructions, in Leviticus 23:26-32, we read about the Day of Atonement. The Jewish people are called upon to afflict their souls on that day. It is a Sabbath day, but like no other Sabbath. The Scriptures add the admonition that whoever does any servile work on the Day of Atonement that soul will be destroyed from among the people (Leviticus 23:30). Twice within the six verses that describe the Day of Atonement we are told to afflict our souls. When the holiday is referred to in Isaiah it is called a *"day for a man to afflict his soul"* (Isaiah 58:5).

The chief characteristic of the Day of Atonement is affliction. In Hosea we read about the Lord coming from heaven to earth. The Lord will not return until Israel acknowledges her offence (Hosea 5:15). The passage continues to speak about the nation being restored to God and says, *"in their affliction they will earnestly seek me."*[26] The affliction refers to the great tribulation and it is called the time of Jacob's trouble in Jeremiah 30:7.

Some of the description of that time includes men travailing in pain as if they were bearing children. The ashen white faces and the anguish of travail that is described in Jeremiah 30:6 remind us of the Jewish community, as they would fast in angst on Yom Kippur.[27]

Jeremiah 30:7 reads, *"Alas! For that day is great, so that none is like it;And it is the time of Jacob's trouble, but he shall be saved out of it."* Israel is saved through the tribulation. The affliction from the tribulation causes Israel to seek God (Hosea 5:15) and to look upon the one whom they pierced (Zechariah 12:10). It is ironic as the tradition teaches that afflicting one's soul will result in salvation and Yom Kippur pictures the time when the nation of Israel will be saved through affliction. The holiday of Yom Kippur is the shadow and the event in time that casts the shadow is Israel's tribulation.

The final Levitical feast is the Feast of Tabernacles or Booths. The holiday is called Succoth from the Hebrew. All those who are born Israelites are instructed to dwell in booths for seven days (Leviticus 23:42). The holiday of Succoth is to remind the Jewish people of the time they dwelled in booths when God brought them out of the land of Egypt (Leviticus 23:43).

The time that Israel spent in the wilderness under God's supervision, provision and protection is a picture of the kingdom age. When the nation was in the wilderness the Lord protected them from evil and prepared them to enter the land of Canaan. Israel is often a type of the eternal state. As the millennium prepares us for heaven the tabernacle experience prepared Israel to live in the land. The thousand-year reign of Christ is the reality; the shadow is the Feast of Tabernacles.

As the first four spring feasts pre-picture the first advent of the Messiah the last three autumn feasts correspond with the aspects of the Second Coming.

Leviticus 23:22	Field-Gap	Church Age
Leviticus 23:23-25	Feast of Trumpets	Rapture
Leviticus 23:26-32	Day of Atonement	Tribulation
Leviticus 23:15-21	Tabernacles	Millennium

Each of the seven feasts pictures some aspect of the ministry and the body of the Lord Jesus. The order of the feasts corresponds precisely with the order that the events actually occur in the history of the Lord and the Church only if the rapture occurs before the tribulation. If the rapture occurs at any other time the language of Colossians 2:16-17 becomes meaningless and the order of the feasts is pointless and insignificant.

Message From Revelation

When we think of the Book of Revelation we naturally reflect on future events. And well we should, as the emphasis of the book is clearly prophecy as we read in the very first verse. *"The Revelation of Jesus Christ, which God gave to him to show His servants things which must shortly take place"*[28] (Revelation 1:1). However, the outline declares the subject matter of the book is to be threefold: the past, the present and the future. The content of Revelation might be complicated, but the outline is really quite simple. The Apostle is instructed to *"Write the things which you have seen, and the things which are, and the things which will take place after this."* Revelation 1:19

"The things which you have seen" is an extremely brief segment, which includes the vision that John had already seen in 1:12-18 and portions of Revelation 12. The expression *"things which are,"* refers to the seven churches in Asia Minor. These churches are addressed in chapters 2 and 3. These literal, historic churches existed at the time of the writing of Revelation. The conditions at each of the churches are symbolic and prophetic of an era or an age for the entire Church.[29]

If the seven churches in chapters 2 and 3 of Revelation represent the entire Church age and the seven churches are the, *"things which are,"* then the Church age is *"the things which are"*. The final words in chapter 3 reads, *"hear what the Spirit says to the churches"*. That admonition closes the chapters dealing with the things past and the things present. The long discussion of the future begins in chapter 4. The first words in Chapter 4 are *"After these things"*. After the church age has come to completion the fourth chapter of Revelation begins.

> Revelation 4:1 *"After these things I looked, and behold, a door standing open in heaven. And the first voice which I heard was like a trumpet speaking with me, saying, 'Come up here, and I will show you things which must take place after this."*

This verse clearly separates the past and the present from the future. The Church age ends with an open door in heaven, a voice like a trumpet and the words, *"Come up hither,"* which forces us to think upon the events that take place at the rapture. If the Scriptures were not trying to teach a pre-tribulation position, why would we read about a voice, the mention of a trumpet, the open door in heaven and the call to come up?

The second verse of Revelation 4 begins with the word, *"immediately"*. The rapture is a sudden event that takes place *"in a moment, in the twinkling of an eye"*.[30]

When John arrives in heaven he encounters 24 elders. The word translated *elder* is the Greek word "presbuteros" and it is used 66 times in the New Testament. In the Gospels the word is used to refer to members of the Sanhedrin. Once the Church is established the word is used to describe ministers and deacons, preaching and business elders of the local churches. It is never used of angels.

The elders that John meets in heaven are distinguished from the angels in Revelation 5:11. John heard the voice of many angels and he heard the voice of the 24 elders. These elders wear crowns and sit on thrones. Crowns and thrones are promised to the Church in several passages (Revelation 2:10, 3:21, 20:4, Matthew 19:28, 1 Corinthians 9:25-27, 2 Timothy 4:8). Angels are never seen with crowns and are only mentioned in connection with thrones once in the Scriptures.[31]

The 24 elders are reported to be wearing white raiment. In the book of Revelation the only people who wear white are believers in heaven and the Lord Himself[32]. The twenty-four elders in Revelation 5:9 sing a song, praising the Lord for their redemption. These elders are redeemed men who are in heaven on thrones in white raiment throughout the entire tribulation. Their presence in heaven proves the Lord has raised the church before the tribulation began.

Once the Church has been raised in Revelation chapter 4, we never see the Church on earth again until the kingdom age begins. On earth we see Jewish believers being separated out. In the Church age there is no distinction between the Jew and the Gentile, but the great tribulation is not the Church age.

I know so many of us desire to go through the great tribulation, but we just cannot. It just is not our calling. I know that we are a most unusual civilization. The American Christian of our generation has escaped persecution and we feel guilty about it. We read Fox's "Book of Martyrs" and we cringe with horror and recoil with shame. Our brothers who have gone before us were honored to live lives worthy of our faith. They died after they were hunted and persecuted for Jesus holy name.

We die from ulcers and cancers caused by rich foods and credit card debts. Most of us will never know persecution because most of us will back down from our faith to avoid being ridiculed. I do not know if our affluent society is a blessing or a curse. I sometimes think that if we were called upon to die for Jesus we would be willing to do so. However, living for Jesus moment-by-moment is too demanding. We apparently have too much and cannot afford to give what we can in the way of service and sacrifice for the Lord. So we feel guilty. We want to expunge our guilt and we want to suffer.

The horrors of the tribulation seem to provide for us the opportunity to join the great crowd of witnesses (Hebrews 12:1) that have gone before us. In the tribulation we can suffer as we think we ought. The belief in the pre-tribulation rapture is not an attempt to avoid suffering. The truth is if we want to suffer, we will just have to put more pepperoni and extra cheese on our pizza. But the Lord is dealing with us according to His marvelous grace. We will not get what we deserve. He has already determined to spare us. As we already cited, the Lord has promised to deliver us from the wrath to come.[33]

As we look at the tribulation, the promise of deliverance comes into question. In Revelation 13:7, we read about a beast that is given power *"to make war with the saints and to overcome them"*. Repeatedly we read about those that have been martyred for their faith during the tribulation. The believers in the tribulation are not delivered. In order for the promise of deliverance to make any sense, it must have been given to the Church and the Church will be delivered from the tribulation at the rapture, which comes before the tribulation begins.

Message From The Kingdom Age

In Isaiah 65:20-25 we read a depiction of the millennial kingdom. In the Kingdom there will be death. This is clearly taught as we read about a child dying at age one hundred (Isaiah 65:20).

Now those who want to go through the tribulation, have to believe that the rapture will occur at the end of the tribulation. But at the end of the tribulation the unbelievers are taken away in judgment. Only believers will enter into the joy of the Lord.

As we mentioned earlier, there are only two kinds of believers, those who are living and those who are dead. Both are raised and translated to receive spiritual bodies. This translation of the church is universal.
1 Corinthians 15:51 assures us, *"We shall not all sleep, but we shall all be changed"*.

Now we have all been changed and we enter the kingdom in spiritual bodies. Who is going to die? How can we die? The enemy, death, is swallowed up in our victory!

Isaiah 65 continues to describe people building houses and living in them. We read about kingdom inhabitants planting the vineyards that produce the fruit that they themselves will eat. The people in the kingdom are described to live as long as trees. There is a picture of universal prosperity.

Verse 23 even makes mention of their offspring. The believers who enter the kingdom will be bearing children. How can believers, after the rapture, after the translation and after putting on incorruptible bodies, possibly continue to have children? The answer is simple, they cannot.

The rapture must have occurred years earlier. That chronology will allow people time to get saved during the tribulation. The believers who endure to the end of the great tribulation will enter into the joy of the Lord in physical bodies. They will build homes, plant vineyards, live in the homes they have built, eat the fruit of their vineyards and they will have children.

At the end of the tribulation, Satan will be loosed and is set free to deceive the nations. He gathers an army of unbelievers to wage a final, universal rebellion against the Lord. If the kingdom begins with all believers who have been translated, then who is being deceived? If we can still be tricked into rebelling against God after living in spiritual bodies for a thousand years, can we ever be safe?

Of course we can be safe. We are secure in Christ. The people who are deceived at the end of the kingdom are the children of the physical bodied saints who entered the kingdom at the end of the tribulation. These believers could not have experienced the translation of the rapture. The rapture would have to have occurred earlier. To believe the Church will go through the tribulation is to throw out the kingdom promises and the future for Israel.

CHAPTER THREE

Signs

> Matthew 24: 3-4, *"Now as He sat on the Mount of Olives, the disciples came to Him privately, saying, 'Tell us, when will these things be? And what will be the sign of Your coming, and of the end of the age?' And Jesus answered and said to them: 'Take heed that no one deceives you. For many will come in My name, saying, "I am the Christ," and will deceive many.'"*

False Messiahs

A sign is visible and so distinct that it enables those who see it to draw a specific conclusion with certainty. The purpose of such a sign is to confirm the identity of a person or event. The first sign that Jesus speaks of is a warning about a multitude of false messiahs that will be successful in deceiving many. These false messiahs, who appear on the scene, cannot be claimants to David's throne. They cannot be professing themselves to be "The Messiah" because they come in Jesus' name.

To recognize who these deceivers are we must understand what the term "Christ" means.[1] False christs, who come in Jesus' name, are phony prophets, lying kings and evil priests. Pseudo Christian leaders that will arrive on the scene in the last days and begin a program of deception that will lead society to the place that, when Satan himself stands up to be worshipped, the world will be prepared to receive him. Certainly all soccer fans will be ready.

Today the prophets are the religious leaders and the kings are the political rulers. The difficulty comes in trying to identify the modern day priests. The priests of today are the philosophers and psychologists. The philosophers shape the values of our society and the psychologists minister to the behavioral problems of the individual.

For a thousand years the priests were the agents of the Roman Catholic Church. They established the philosophy for all of Europe. They controlled the way men thought and kept their constituency in darkness. Religions like Catholicism and Islam are illogical. They are inconsistent with their own convictions. These religious systems could not prevail in a theatre of fair debate, so they cannot allow for a mutual exchange of ideas. Hence they keep the people oppressed and hold them in fear.

The Protestant Reformation encouraged people to search the Scriptures for themselves. The freedom to search for truth produced new churches, a newfound theology and a new, enlightened world for those who searched the Scriptures.

Unfortunately that same liberty produced havoc in the hearts of men under the tutelage of the false messiahs. I tried to discover who these false messiahs might be.

Before I began working with the rapid information available via the Internet, every year I would purchase the "Information Please Almanac". The almanac had a special feature section called "Ideas and Beliefs" which lists the significant ideas and beliefs that people have held during different periods of history. I looked up every single reference to discover when they were introduced into our civilization.

Many ideas predate the statement that Jesus made regarding the introduction of false messiahs. Any philosophy, religion, or political system that was in existence at the time of Christ could not possibly be one that he was predicting. I then charted the ones that came into existence after the time of Jesus by date. The results were astonishing. From the time of Jesus forward very little original thought was brought into the world for centuries.

According to the almanac there was not a single new idea or belief in the 1st, 7th, 9th, 10th and 12th centuries. There was one new

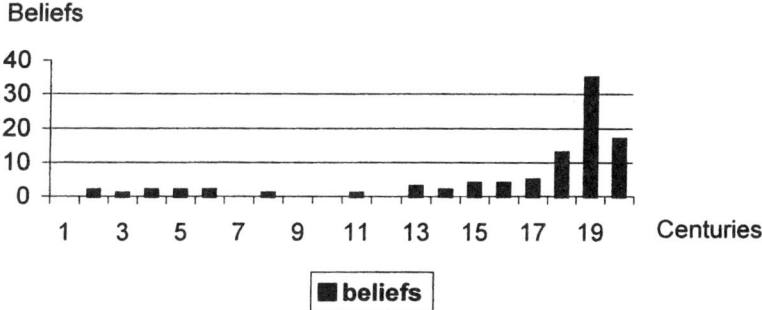

belief added in each of the 3rd, 8th and 11th centuries. There were two new beliefs introduced in each of the 2nd, 4th, 5th, 6th and 14th centuries. Three new beliefs entered in the 13th century and four were added in the 15th and 16th centuries. Five new beliefs date back to the 17th century and then we go off the charts for the next couple of hundred years. Thirteen new beliefs commenced in the 18th century, followed by thirty-five in the 19th and seventeen in the 20th. More new ideas and beliefs entered our world in the past three hundred years then in the 17 hundred years before them. For 1700 years we saw only 24 new ideas and beliefs, yet in the past 300 years there have been 65.

After categorizing the new ideas by date, I then classified them into three groups - psychological, political and religious; the three areas where the priests, kings and prophets were anointed in Biblical times. From the end of the 18th until the beginning of the 20th century a phenomenal number of new ideas and beliefs invaded the planet.

(Priests) Psychological	(Kings) Political	(Prophets) Religious
Romantism - 1772	Illuminati - 1776	Unitarianism - 1813
Utilitarinism - 1806	Capitalism - 1790	Christadelphians - 1840
Associationism - 1806	Malthusianism - 1798	Adventist - 1844
Existentialism - 1850	Anti Semitism – 1816-1882	Mormons - 1846
Dialetic Materialism - 1850	Marxism - 1848	Spiritualism - 1847
Eugenics - 1850	Nihilism - 1862	Bahai Faith - 1850
Psycho analysis - 1856	Communism - 1870	Anglican Communion - 1867
Orgonomy - 1897	Trotskyism - 1879-1940	Theosophy - 1875
Empiricism - 1899	Fabian Society - 1884	Christian Science - 1879
Rationalism - 1899	Facism - 1914	Jehovah's Witness - 1879
Adlerian Psychology - 1911	Nazism - 1914	Golden Dawn Society - 1887
Analytical Psychology - 1911		Modernism - 1893
Behaviorism - 1914		Pentecostalism - 1901
Vitalism - 1915		

These ideas speak as if they had the authority of God, but they are false messiahs and are not truly anointed. The false priests undermine the belief in and the need for God. They teach that man is basically good and does not need to be redeemed. The false kings introduce governments and political systems that govern without God while the false prophets introduce religions that undermine the authority of the Scriptures. These false messiahs cajole our society towards accepting the rule of the ultimate false messiah and their presence on the scene is a sign of the times that we live in.

False Priests

Romanticism - 1772

When I went to college, we studied the overwhelming impact that Romanticism had on our world. I marvel that the subject seems to have been eliminated from the current curriculum. Apparently, romanticism is no longer an outside movement that needs to be studied. It is the dynamic force that drives our art, literature, science, religion, economics and politics.

Thomas Paine called the period when men broke free from religious thinking, "The Age of Reason." The thinking of that time was called "Enlightenment." The Enlightenment thinkers saw the world as being one of rational order. The Enlightenment mantra was that the natural world was rationally ordered and therefore could be analyzed and understood through human reason. Primarily, Romanticism is the rejection of Enlightenment with its emphasis upon human reason.

Romanticism applauds instinct and intuition over logic and observations. It approves of emotions, feelings and the brilliance of creativity. It delights in legends from foreign lands, other cultures and the fantasy world of man's imagination. Romanticism takes delight in sights, sounds and feelings. The disdain for rational thought is clearly seen in an early poem.

"One impulse from a vernal wood
May teach you more of man,
Of moral evil and of good
Than all the sages can.

Are We There Yet?

> *Sweet is the lore which Nature brings;*
> *Our meddling intellect Misshapes the beauteous forms of things,*
> *We murder to dissect enough of Science and of Art;*
> *Close up those barren leaves; Come forth and bring with you a heart That watches and receives*[2].

Christianity is based in objective reality and insists on absolutes. Romanticism is the philosophical opposite of the revealed faith. Christianity promotes submission to authority while Romanticism endorses revolution. The Christian church is the basis for community, family and fellowship. Romanticism, with the emphasis of feeling over facts encourages individuality since feelings are personal and cannot be shared.

The priesthood of Romanticism is a giant foundational step that paves the path away from the straight and narrow to the wide road that leads to destruction. Romanticism was foisted upon this generation through the school system. We were all introduced to the philosophy through the mandatory reading of such works as the Hermann Hesse novel, "Steppenwolf" and J.D. Salinger's "Catcher in the Rye".

More than two hundred years later, the dynamism of this philosophy has not diminished though it has taken some strange twists and contradictory turns.

One of the results is nationalism. Nationalism is really an extension of the emphasis on self. The exaltation of self elevates culture, language and arts, over faith. This sentiment emerges in France, Germany and Italy and has crossed over the Atlantic to our shores. It breaks down the universal bond of the body of believers.

An extension of nationalism is ethnicity, which has a focus on the cohesiveness of a people with common tribal roots. During the 19th century there was a strong cultural movement among the people of Eastern Europe that called for the unity of Slavic peoples. In Germany the Nazi slogan was "One nation, one people, one leader."

In the United States we had the civil rights movement that produced slogans like "black power' and "black is beautiful", which bred the reaction of "white power." Again the church is further divided and the second birth takes a back seat to one's first birth.

With the removal of absolutes Romanticism effected politics in two different directions. The void left people looking for something to count on; something strong and dependable. This facilitated the rise to power of the dictators that governed from both the right and the left extremes. The absence of absolutes also removed the respect for formally assumed powers. The divine right of kings becomes obsolete and people demand a greater role in government.

Romanticism was the thinking behind the French revolution, the United States constitution and the socialistic ideals of the Communist party. One of the more obnoxious results of Romanticism is that two people can have mutually exclusive, opposing points of view and they can both be right.

In my world one, if not both, must be incorrect since I deal in objective reality. Unfortunately our world is becoming more influenced by individualism and subjectivity. There is an expression "hopelessly romantic," which defines one without objective reality, without God and therefore without hope (Ephesians 2:12). The expression should probably be "hopeless romanticism".

Utilitarianism - 1806

Utilitarianism is a theory that defines the moral correctness of an act by the consequences. English philosophers James Mill and John Stuart Mill developed the philosophy in the 1800's. Utilitarians believe in situation ethics. What makes an act morally right is that it leads to the best consequences. The Utilitarian would discard all religious rules like the Ten Commandments and replace them with a flexible code that allowed people to perform whatever act would have the best results.

One difficulty is in defining the word "best". Without any absolutes it is impossible to choose between pleasure, happiness, knowledge, love or freedom as the ultimate good. Early proponents tried to devise a method to measure the value of actions. They extended this theory to politics, claiming that government should promote the well being of its citizens.

Utilitarianism is an early form of cost/benefit analysis, a method now often used in politics and economics. It isn't difficult to see the influence this philosophy has left. Today's political parties have defined the greatest good as the most popular idea. They set their platforms on the basis of the results of surveys.

Corporations have determined that the greatest good is the bottom line. The safety of a product is ignored, the protection of workers is neglected and environmental concerns are overlooked. Doing the right thing is now defined in terms of results.

Recently a young Christian woman determined it would be best to divorce her husband. The words, "in sickness and in health, for better and for worse, till death do us part" had become insignificant to her. The marriage vows that she made before God were disregarded. Biblical principles clearly taught in the Scriptures were not governing her life. Her decisions were being made on the basis of utilitarianism and even within the confines of this unbiblical theology, her definition of the "greatest good" was decadent. There seemed to be no interest in God's glory, or concern for the interest of the children, or the testimony of the home. For her the greatest good was personal convenience.

Many Christians do not consider the worth of the Creator, they only consider the cost of obedience. We are to determine the rightness of an act on the basis of the authority of God's word rather than the outcome.

Associationism - 1806

The aforementioned John Stuart Mill (1806-1873) also worked on the psychological theory of Associationism. The almanac described the theory as follows:

> *"Accepted the association of ideas as the fundamental principle in mental life...mental activity was nothing but the association of 'ideas' conceived of as units of both thought and feeling-the emotion of anger or the perception of a chair were both ideas and apart from the self did not exist. Personality was simply a series of these units coming and going, adding to or cancelling (sic) each other out, in accordance with rigid and mechanistic scientific views."*[3]

I have met people who say, "I wish I could believe". The psychological theory of Associationism allows for that kind of thinking. In Christianity we are responsible for our thoughts and our conclusions. We are commanded to control our thoughts (2 Corinthians 10:5).[4] The philosophy of Associationism not only removes human responsibility, but it also presents us as helpless victims of the things that haphazardly enter our minds.

Existentialism - 1850

Remember, we did not select these trends on the basis of how wicked they might be, but we simply copied them out of the almanac on the basis of when they were introduced into the world.

Existentialism is in some ways the philosophical opposite of Associationism. Where Associationism sees man as an extension of the helpless plants and animals from which he evolved, Existentialism recognizes that man is different. Unlike the flowers man can choose, man can think. Possibly the best known of those who promoted existentialist themes was Kierkegaard, who wrote from a Christian perspective. Atheists like Albert Camus and Jean-Paul Sartre also supported the view.

Are We There Yet?

Because man is free to choose, the existentialist lives in a world that is uncertain. According to the Existentialist, the world does not always make sense, as we live in a world that may be filled with uncertainty. Where actions based upon the best-laid plans of individuals and societies often have an unintended effect. Dostoevski said that there are no underlying patterns in the universe that can be perceived by everyone. For him the world was unpredictable and capricious.

Atheistic Existentialism produces a universe without a designer. Man by the very nature of his existence becomes the designer for the world to come. Existentialism has influenced some 20th century theologians like Karl Barth, Paul Tillich and Rudolph Bultmann.

Dialectic Materialism - 1850

The most famous name associated with Dialectic Materialism is that of Karl Marx, who along with Friedrich Engels developed this philosophy, which became the philosophical basis for Marxism and Communism.

Dialectics is an ancient system of dialogue employed by Socrates in which philosophical disputes could be resolved. A thesis would be proposed and then an opposing position called the anti-thesis would be presented. The two positions would be argued until a synthesis could be reached. The synthesis becomes the new thesis, which would be followed by a new anti-thesis.

This continued introduction of successive contradiction was applied to civilizations. The application is made within the light of Darwin's theories of evolution. Marx believed that societies were evolving through a process from thesis to anti-thesis to synthesis. The anti-thesis would be revolution.

Eugenics - 1850

The word eugenics comes from a Greek word that literally means "wellborn". Some of the ideas can be seen in antiquity in Plato's republic, but the true philosophy was born in the 19th century.

In 1833 a British scientist named Francis Galton coined the term eugenics. Galton was a cousin of Charles Darwin and the theory of evolution was obviously a great influence on him. In a book published in 1869, Galton suggested that man should control his own evolutionary process. He presented the practicality of producing gifted and influential men by judiciously arranging marriages to suitable wives for several successive generations.

Galton may have been one of the earliest, but he certainly was not alone in his thinking. In 1872 Victoria Woodhull became the first woman to be nominated for president by a political party. This feminist leader believed that if superior people are to be desired, they must be bred; and if imbeciles, criminals, paupers and the otherwise unfit are undesirable citizens, they must not be bred.

Eugenics became a sweeping and highly destructive movement to improve the human race from the late l9th century through the end of World War II in 1945. Many who promoted Eugenics were outside the scientific community. One very influential man was a British mathematician named Karl Pearson. Pearson emphasized that certain social classes and races were superior to others. Pearson and his followers totally ignored the influence of environment in the development of personality and character.

The theories of Pearson eventually led to the discrediting of Eugenics as a scientific discipline in the United States. However they enjoyed early and wide reception and greatly influenced the thinking of the Nazi party.

In Nazi Germany Adolph Hitler exterminated from 18 to 26 million people and about 40% of this number were Jewish people. These people were murdered in death camps because of the Nazi belief in eugenic theories. Inferior people had to be controlled by the German master race.

During these same years in the United States, many eugenicists supported the sterilization of people considered to be defective. By 1931 sterilization laws had been enacted by 27 States in the United States and by 1935 five other countries had passed similar laws.

Today, anthropologists believe that culture and experience are at the root of behavior. So the emphasis of Eugenics has changed from altering civilization to the control and elimination of disease. Eugenics has been restored to scientific respectability in the world of genetic engineering.

Psychoanalysis - 1856

Psychoanalysis is the product of an Austrian physician named Sigmund Freud. Freudian psychology is so prevalent in our society that the term Freudian slip has become a proverb and everyone is familiar with the terminologies of id, ego and super ego.

Most of us have not been under analysis. However, analysis has shaped our culture. Many actors, directors, producers and writers in the motion picture industry, which is so influential and powerful in the molding of our society, *have* undergone analysis. They speak about it without restraint publicly and openly. It is so commonplace that it has become a source of humor, a regular and reoccurring theme. But, to be funny humor has to have a basis in reality. The reality is that a large percentage of the most popular and authoritative people in our culture is currently relying on the psychoanalytical process to live their lives. For them psychoanalysis has replaced prayer, meditation and confession.

In seminary we were instructed in the various schools of psychology. Most psychology comes under the heading of "Why Psychology." All the psychological systems that employ a variation of Freud's developmental theory would fall into the category of "Why

Psychology". The "Why Psychological" school seeks to explain why you are the way you are.

Freud expounded that we grow through five stages of psychosexual development. Often we get traumatized during one of the developmental stages. The pain of the trauma causes us to repress the experience and that repressed memory can result in neurotic behavior.

Under analysis the psychiatrist or psychologist attempts to determine when the trauma occurred so the patient can discover why they are the way they are. Under psychoanalysis it might be reassuring to discover that your neurosis is normal for your circumstances. The downside is that understanding why will do nothing to correct your behavior. Freud saw guilt as paranoia. The problem is that sometimes we are guilty.

The second kind of psychology we studied was affectionately referred to as "What Psychology". This discipline focuses on behavior. The three questions asked are what did you do? What should you have done? And what are you going to do about it?

Freud, with all his dream analyzing, his free association (which probably cost $100 an hour) and his developmental theories did nothing to effect a single behavioral change since he did not believe in depravity.

Freud has a vast number of followers, who do not recognize the basic reality of man's nature. Carl Young, Alfred Adler, Otto Rank blame everything from social experience, to tall parents, or to birth order, but man is never to blame.

A second generation of practitioners referred to as neo-Freudians include names like Eric Fromm, Karen Horney, Eric Erikson, Sullivan and Klein to name just a few. They add to the theories, alter the ideas and pass the concepts on to the next generation.

A new generation of counselors and physicians practicing psychology and psychiatry are making people feel good about themselves by blaming environment, parents and siblings for their problems. Training our society to believe that they are without sin and without responsibility.

Orgonomy - 1897

Orgonomy is a little known theory that was advanced by one of the many pupils of Sigmund Freud, a German psychiatrist named Wilhelm Reich. Reich believed that all living beings were permeated by a force field, which he termed the "orgone." According to Reich the orgone could be photographed and measured with a Geiger counter. Reich was expelled from Germany because of his verbal opposition to the Nazi party.

He came to America and found a large following for his bizarre views. He taught that the orgone was most successfully transmitted throughout the body through sexual intercourse. Reich contributed to the obsession with sexuality in our culture and he promoted the idea of sex as a panacea.

Empiricism - 1899

Empiricism is a school of philosophy that says that if a man wants to find out what the universe is like, the only correct way is to gather the data himself. Only information that can be discovered through one's own senses is valid. English philosophers George Berkeley, John Locke and David Hume held to this view. Empiricism would ignore or deny the value of any information beyond ones own observations. If you do not see, or touch, or hear a Supreme Being then, according to Empiricism, a Supreme Being does not exist. Empiricism would be in opposition to faith since *"faith is the evidence of things not seen"* (Hebrews 11:1).

Rationalism - 1899

Rationalism is the treatment of reason as the ultimate authority in religion. Any doctrine that is not consistent with reason or logic would be rejected. Rationalism is anti religious. Organizations like the Secular Society, the National Secular Society and the Rationalist Press Association promote rationalism as well as the causes of atheism and agnosticism. Although our faith is certainly reasonable and cogent it is based on revelation; not rationalization. The Scriptures show the impossibility of comprehension through human reasoning by revealing the grand difference between our thoughts and God's thoughts. His ways are just too high for us to understand through unaided logic (Isaiah 55:8-9).

Adlerian Psychology - 1911

Alfred Adler and Carl Jung broke away from Freud thinking that he overemphasized the influence of sexuality. Adler later separated from Jung and started his own school.

Adler taught that the driving force was not sex, but the issue of compensation. Children begin life feeling inferior to the parents or to the older and perhaps bullying siblings. This sense of inferiority then drives us to compensate by excelling in some area of life. Those of us who cannot excel or at least become competent then become neurotic. We flee from reality into a realm where we can deal with the inferiority. Adler referred to it as the unconscious flight into illness.

As far as the "Why Psychologists" are concerned, Adler was certainly one of the more insightful. His views are reflected among accepted Christian psychologists. However, "Why Psychology" is still limited to defining problems and does not deal in solving problems. Adlerian psychology also is seeking to solve the wrong problem. Adler ignored the Scriptures and the true nature of man. Adler denied the doctrine of depravity and never dealt with man's responsibility.

Analytical Psychology 1911

Carl Jung started this school when Adler and he separated. Jung stressed the unconscious mind and repressed memories or socially unaccepted emotions. Also he believed that deep in the unconscious mind of man remain ancient ways of thought inherited from centuries past. As all the other versions of "Why Psychology" Analytical Psychology only seeks to apologize and explain the causes for problems, rather than solving problems. This is another influence that discourages a focus on personal responsibility.

Behaviorism - 1914

Behaviorism is a reaction to the focus on human thought that prevailed in psychology. John B. Watson introduced behaviorism and argued that thoughts are unscientific since they cannot be observed or measured. Behavior, however, can be observed and is therefore more scientific. Watson also believed that all behavior is learned.

Behaviorism became a major thrust of American psychology for the first half of the 20th century. Psychologists such as Clark L. Hull at Yale University and B.F. Skinner at Harvard argued that human thought is an inference from behavior and that all psychology could, or should, be concerned only with behavior.

A major influence in turning American psychology to behaviorism came from the work of the Russian physiologist Ivan Pavlov. Pavlov discovered what he called the conditioned reflex. Pavlov observed that when he paired a neutral (conditioned) stimulus such as a buzzer with a natural (unconditioned) stimulus such as food, the reflex response to the food, salivation, eventually came to be elicited by the buzzer. Pavlov called the response to the conditioned stimulus a conditioned reflex.

Pavlov's psychology became the official dogma of the Communist party. Behavior can be controlled and people are not thinking souls but responding animals. Where Jung saw depths in the unconscious mind that tie us to the past, the behaviorist sees man as an advanced animal responding to stimuli. The behaviorist cannot understand people acting out of love or sacrifice. The behaviorist cannot comprehend faith, courage or commitment and in America behaviorists greatly affected the education system.

Vitalism - 1915

The rationalist thinker E.M. Joad held to this belief. Vitalism sees evolution as a fact. Also it sees evolution as the work of an artist and is creative and unpredictable. It is interesting to me that they recognize design, but ignore the designer. They say that all behavior is due at least in part to a vital principle which cannot be explained in terms of physics or chemistry. Vitalism is the last of the psychological and philosophical influences to enter our world during the period of the invasion of the false messiahs.

For 17 centuries only 29 new ideas were introduced to our world. Then in the 140 years from 1775 to 1915, there was an avalanche of ideas in the areas of philosophy, psychology, government and religion.

In philosophy these ideas stress subjective thinking and deny the existence of objective reality. They reject religion and revelation. They are atheistic and believe in evolution.

In psychology they reject the concept of sin and remove personal responsibility. Some schools of thought see man as the ultimate animal in the evolutionary scale; an animal that can be controlled through the proper set of stimuli. Others see man as a complex product of failed experiences causing neurotic behavior. These psychological schools do not recognize the need for forgiveness, the old sin nature or the reality of the Holy Spirit.

False Kings

Illuminati - 1776

In 1776 Adam Weishaupt, a Bavarian professor, established a secret society to combat superstition and ignorance. He founded the Illuminati for rational enlightenment and the regeneration of the world. The Iilluminati attempted to penetrate the Masonic lodges for subversive purposes. The order spread to Austria, Italy and Hungary. It was condemned by the Roman Catholic Church and was supposedly dissolved by the Bavarian government in 1785.

Capitalism - 1790

Capitalism is the name that was coined in the late 18th century for an economic system that began to develop a century earlier. Other names for this system are *free market economy* and *free enterprise*. The word "capital" originally referred to the money, land, buildings and machinery that are needed to operate a factory or farm. The capitalist is the individual who supplies the resources.

The other two terms both include the word free. It is freedom that characterizes the system. The implication is that people have individual liberty and the right to own property. In a capitalistic society people must also have the right to do what they wish with their property. These freedoms set capitalism apart from all other kinds of economic arrangements. In other systems individual freedoms and property are sacrificed for the good of the state. In capitalism the individual can produce with his property whatever goods or services he chooses and the consumer has the right to choose what to purchase.

Capitalism believes that in a free market without controls, the laws of supply and demand will naturally establish equitable prices and wages. Capitalism requires a free citizenry to function. It is a good economic system, but it tends to produce a materialistic focus and an avarice society.

Malthusianism - 1798

Malthusianism is a theory that a man named Malthus advanced in an essay on populations. He was one of the earliest alarmists to be concerned with an over-populated planet. His apprehension was that a population that increases in a geometric ratio, if left unchecked, will, eventually, outrun subsistence increasing in an arithmetical ratio.[5]

The problem was clearly presented; the possible solutions were not. A century later Hitler had suggested one possible solution and today the abortionist suggests a second one.

Marxism - 1848

Karl Marx and I have several things in common. We both were born into Jewish homes. Of course he was born in 1818, some 130 years earlier than my birth. Karl's grandfather was a rabbi, but his father was a lawyer who had his entire family baptized for business and social reasons. So both of us are Jewish men who have been baptized.

During his lifetime Marx was known only to a small group of revolutionaries and socialists. The books he wrote were largely ignored at the time. His books are now considered by Communists all over the world to be the source of absolute truth on matters of economics, philosophy and politics. In fact, most modern socialists base their doctrines on Marx's theories. Just like Marx, the books I have written are for the most part largely ignored. Also, most of our close friends are revolutionaries and socialists.

Marx studied law at Bonn and philosophy at the University of Berlin. While in Berlin he became acquainted with the philosophy of Wilhelm Friedrich Hegel. At 24 he became editor of a paper in

Are We There Yet?

Cologne, Germany. His radical ideas soon got him into censorship trouble and he went to Paris, partly to escape arrest. Marx was expelled from Paris in 1845, returned in 1849 and was expelled again. Then Marx went to London where he made his home for the remaining 34 years of his life.

He was never very successful and lived in poverty for most of his life. Which is another fact that we have in common. Marx was a family man devoted to his wife and children. He would spend most of his time studying in the British museum. Marx had an uncompromising nature and alienated most would be friends. He outlived his wife and four of his six children.

His one true ally, a textile manufacturer named Engels, spoke to eight people at Marx's funeral. He worked with Marx on a document called "Manifesto of the Communist Party" which was published in 1848. The ideas expressed in the original document were later expanded upon in the major work "Das Kapital" which first appeared in 1867.

Marx based his theories on what he believed to be the scientific evidence of history. He searched the past for proof of the continual class struggle between the middle-class exploiters (the bourgeoisie) and the oppressed working people (the proletariat). The final struggle, he predicted, would lead to the overthrow of capitalism and its supporters. He believed a classless society would then emerge and there would thus be no more revolutions.

Marx hoped that governments would wither away and that men would live by the rule of "from each according to his ability; to each according to his needs". It is a lovely sentiment. Unfortunately, since man is depraved it serves better as a slogan on a greeting card than it does as a realistic rule of society.

Anti-Semitism - 1862

Anti-Semitism is simply stated as hatred of Jews. Technically it is an incorrect term since Semites would include other ethnic groups besides Jewish people. However, when we are speaking of a universal movement of such uncanny and unspeakable evil, a movement that is so horribly wrong on so many levels, you tend to ignore the incorrect use of vocabulary.

Anti-Semitism has been around since the time of Pharaoh. It was practiced by the Assyrians and Babylonians and became national policy for the Persians. It has been a favorite pastime and policy of the Roman Catholic Church and was one of the few things that Christianity and Islam could heartily agree on.

Anti-Semitism was truly perfected under the Russian Czars giving way for the need of a name of its own. The actual term was coined during the end of the nineteenth century. Previously, anti-Semitism was based on religious prejudice. This new movement is motivated by economic and political conditions and is fueled by pseudo scientific theories. Early documents that used the term and actually attempted a rationale for the hatred appeared circa 1850, written by such men as Gobineau and Houston Stewart Chamberlain. It was openly discussed as a viable, national policy and was unabashedly promoted, not just understood or defended. These guys did not even have the decency to wear sheets over their heads.

The first pogroms were spawned in 1882 in Russia and later spread to Hungary[6] The pogroms of 1903 and 1905 slaughtered scores of thousands of Jewish people.

"Protocols of the Elders of Zion" was first published in 1905.[7] Although the document was a clumsy and obvious fraud, it was instantly and universally embraced. Translated and published throughout all of Europe, Asia, North America and South America, it would have been a hit in Africa too, but at the time most third world nations and nomadic Islamic tribes were illiterate. The "Protocols" were used to justify pogroms, but they also fueled the fires for the future Nazi policies of Jewish extinction. It is so comforting to see such good usage of literature.

Nihilism - 1862

In philosophy, Nihilism refers to the denial of the existence of any basis for knowledge or truth. It often refers to the overall rejection of any belief in morality or religion. In ethics it is the belief that there is no purpose or meaning in life. These two concepts combine to form the political doctrine that all existing social, political and economic institutions must be totally eradicated to allow for the formation of new institutions.

The term originated in the reign of Tsar Alexander II who is credited with liberating the serfs. It later became identified with the movement in Russia which advocated revolutionary reform and attempted to carry it out through the use of terrorism and assassination. Nihilism was popularized in the writings of Friedrich Nietzsche 1844-1900. Nietzsche is more pessimistic than a Philadelphia Phillies fan during the playoffs.[8]

Communism - 1870

Communism is the product of unbiblical philosophies and the ungodly views of government which preceded it. The communist goal is a society in which the workers of the world own all the land, the factories and the machinery. The first step towards this utopia would be overthrow and elimination of the current government. Then a temporary and transitional despot would be established who would have total control of the economy. The failure has always been that the temporary tyrant seems to fail to relinquish his own absolute powers and the transition never occurs. It was almost as if the tyrant himself was a depraved sinner.

When Lenin came into power in Russia in 1917 he realized the inability of the communist system to motivate a population to fully utilize the resources. It was almost as if the people were depraved sinners who would only work for themselves and not for society. Lenin attempted multiple experiments which all failed. The workable economy of Russia was all but demolished. He died in 1924 in frustration before a feasible system could be established.

His successor, Joseph Stalin, created the Communist State and assumed the role of a god. He became one of the most ruthless dictators the world had ever known. He took control of all agriculture, industry, arts, science, sports, entertainment, media and religion. The state bureaucracy governed every aspect of society. It decided what should be produced, how much and at what price. All wages and prices were subject to government control. In return, the people got a welfare-state and complete security from the cradle to the grave. Hospitalization, education, housing and pension plans were all guaranteed by the state, as were jobs. The people, in turn, gave up every vestige of freedom.

To insure the system worked, his commands had to be obeyed. Stalin employed a vast network of secret police. A large system of prison camps was built to accommodate all those accused of subverting the state. Under Stalin millions of people were murdered. Absolute control had to be maintained. Information about growing economic freedoms under capitalism had to be subverted.

Communism relies on expansionism. The seeds of discord and revolution must be sown in neighboring nations and in budding nations around the world.

Fabian Society - 1884

In 1848, the year of the Communist Manifesto, Europe was in revolt. In most European nations workers and intellectuals were involved in bloody revolutions against the ruling classes. However, although communism began in England it never became an important movement there because of the strong and lasting sway of Christianity.

Beginning with "The Great Awakening" under Wesley, Christian influence continued to grow due to the dynamic preaching of men like Charles Haddon Spurgeon, Alexander Whyte, F.B. Meyer, Alexander MacClaren, Henry Paddon Liddon, Robert William Dale, William Booth and Joseph Parker to name just a few. In a Christian society the worst of the factory abuses were corrected. Wage earners and those who owned factories worshiped alongside each other. Social changes were being brought about gradually through Parliament.

The Fabian Society was founded in 1884 and took its name from a general, who in ancient Rome won a victory over Hannibal by avoiding direct battle. The society was a movement of intellectuals, which included H. G Welles and George Bernard Shaw. It was basically a research institute that provided information for social reform and supported all those who encouraged the gradual establishment of socialistic policies through the parliamentary process.

The Fabian Society believed capitalism was a doomed system and that a change to socialism was inevitable. They explained that the reason all past attempts to develop a Utopian civilization had failed was because they were based on the fallacy that civilizations are static.

They applied the theory of evolution to governmental systems feeling men were rational enough to guide the process of change and to affect their own evolution. They believed that surely, rational men would in time recognize and come to accept a socialistic world and that the violent overthrow of governments was the incorrect way to bring evolution.

Trotskyism - 1924

Trotsky is the assumed name of Lev Bronstein, who was ousted from power by Stalin in 1924. Trotsky argued that the policies of Stalin were excessively nationalistic and contrary to principles of pure international communism. Trotsky was assassinated in Mexico in 1940.

Differences between Trotsky and Lenin seem to be more personal than political or philosophical. However, the movement that used his name continued long after his death. In 1956 there was an uprising in Hungary which was ruthlessly suppressed by Soviet armed forces. This anti-Soviet sentiment produced a rise in the supporters of Trotskyism.

Nazism - 1914

Nazism is the political doctrine of the National Socialist German Worker's party. The subject is divided under various sub-titles such as Barth, Buber, chemical warfare, concentration camps, eugenics, euthanasia, genocide, Judaism, Poland, propaganda and socialism. We know more about who they are and what they did than what they believed. The only clear doctrine is that Nazis are anti-Semites. All neo-Nazis and Nazi organizations have this same single passion.

Fascism - 1914

Fascism is one of the major forms of government today. The name is derived from a Latin word for the symbol of authority in ancient Rome. Fascism, like Communism, held to the concept that the state was supreme above the individual. All individuals must work together for the betterment of the state. The word fascism was first used by Benito Mussolini in Italy to describe the form of government he brought to that nation. The governments of Germany, Japan, South Africa and Argentina have all been Fascist.

Although Communism and Fascism result in dictatorships and the depravation of human rights they really are very different. Dictatorship in Communist governments was supposed to be temporary, the intention being to break the power of capitalism on behalf of the exploited working class.

Fascism, however, embraced capitalism and forged a political alliance with it, working with those who controlled production to provide an improved economic function for the nation. Where Communism was based on philosophical theories, Fascism was merely a means to gain and wield power. Since it did not have a strong base of political beliefs Fascism was flexible where Communism was rigid and could devise policies on a trial and error basis, making up the rules as it went along.

Eventually, Fascism came to base its survival on existing philosophies. The principles of Machiavelli[9] served as the foundation of the government of Italy, while in Germany the chief philosopher was Friedrich Nietzsch. Interestingly, Nietzsche hated the state, but despised democracy even more. The writings of Nietzsche paved the way for the "super man" and his "will to power". [10] [11]

False Prophets

Unitarianism

This is a liberal religious denomination that stresses individual beliefs and reasoning. Unitarianism rejects the doctrine of the triune God and other fixed creeds. The earliest of the organized Unitarian movements appeared in England in 1773. The movement remained influential in New England from the middle of 18th century and in 1961 they merged with the Universalists.[12] The Unitarians faced persecution, shunning and intolerance in England, but found more acceptance in the United States. Many well-known people were openly Unitarian and their faith influenced many through the literature they produced. It pays to advertise. Emerson, Longfellow, Lowell and Oliver Wendell Holmes were all active practicing Unitarians. Unitarianism is one of the earliest evidences of the affects that Romanticism had upon religion. The Bible and all universal absolutes are discarded in favor of individual reasoning.

Christadelphians - 1840

This church started in the late 1840's under John Thomas and its doctrine is another example of the prevailing philosophies in the world influencing religion. Thomas was born in England and came to the United States where he joined the Disciples of Christ.[13] He later became convinced that their doctrine made them the apostate church of the book of Revelation.

Christadelphians reject the doctrine of the triune God and immortality of the soul. They believe that only believers who are baptized by immersion are to live forever and everyone else is annihilated. Eternal condemnation in Hell offends their senses, so the doctrine is ignored. The triune nature of God is illogical, so they just deny it.

These theologies seem to use the methods of dialectics and are influenced by the world. Human reasoning starts in Scripture and then continues out in a linear projection proceeding into logic and further from the truth. This results in heresy for the believer and despair for the lost.

We need to continually return to the Scriptures. Our thinking should be elliptical, not linear, growing in expanding circles that continuously return to the central word for the truth.

Adventists - 1844

Technically all who believe in the Second Coming of Jesus Christ are "Adventists." The term has come to be applied to the followers of the teachings of William Miller. He calculated the return of the Lord to be between March 21, 1843 and March 21, 1844. When the Lord did not return during that time many people left the movement. They recalculated a second date for October 22, 1844. At that time there were between fifty and one hundred thousand Adventists in the country. Hundreds if not thousands of them sold their property, gave away their goods and waited prayerfully for the blessed day. When

Are We There Yet?

October 22, came and passed without an appearance of the Lord, vast numbers left.

The organization then splintered into different groups. The largest of them was the Seventh Day Adventists. Their major doctrinal differences are not related to the Sabbath at all. They believe the sanctuary in Daniel 9 is in heaven and that it was to this heavenly sanctuary that Jesus returned to on October 22, 1844.

A small group of these Adventists began worshiping on Saturday in New Hampshire. The leaders of this movement were Joseph Bates, James White and Ellen Harmon. Ellen Harmon later married James White and became Ellen White.

Adventists believe in soul sleep, eternal life for the saved and eternal destruction by fire for the lost also they believe in keeping the Ten Commandments, hence the observance of the Sabbath, and they abstain from alcohol and tobacco also they believe in prophecy holding to the writings of Ellen White as inspired by the Lord.[14]

Mormons 1846

Most of us have heard of the Mormons. In fact, if you look outside your door you may see two thin, handsome young men dressed in long sleeved white shirts, ties and no jacket. They would be Mormon missionaries and though appearing to be completely sane, they suffer from some inexplicable malady that causes them to become completely delusional in regards to understanding history.

In the 1300's the bacillus pasteurella pestis invaded the continent of Europe through fleas and rodents, resulting in the Bubonic plague and almost half the population of Europe died. In the same manner, in the middle of the 1800's a delusional spirit, working through individuals and having disregard for the Scriptures, invaded the United States and millions of people left the reality of the Word to chase visions and teachings of men.

In Revelation 12 we read about Satan being cast out of heaven. It is probably a tribulation event that has not yet happened, but something did happen in the 1800's and a spirit of deception permeated the air.

Joseph Smith, founder of the Mormon Church, claimed God told him all the existing churches were in error. He was told to reestablish the true church on earth. An angel supposedly led him to discover golden tablets that were left in New York State by a prophet of old. These golden tablets were said to contain the record of an ancient civilization that had lived in America and were said to be the true word of God.

Smith allegedly translated the tablets, which were written in hieroglyphics, into what was called "The Book of Mormon" and returned them to the angel. Of course Joseph Smith did not know hieroglyphics characters so, to aid him in translation the angel also provided Joseph with magical glasses. The spectacles were also returned to the angel.

To accept the teaching of the Church of the Latter Day Saints, the official name for the Mormons, one has to ignore the fields of archaeology and anthropology. One would have to believe that the Lord has allowed His entire church to continue in total darkness for two thousand years. I know the Mormon Tabernacle Choir can do Handle's Messiah with the best of them, but you have to throw your brains out the window to believe in golden tablets and magic glasses. Yet, today there are five differing Mormon sects, the largest of which has over two million members in over six thousand churches. Whatever it is, I do not understand it. Maybe fleas transmit it.

Spiritualism - 1847

The plague of delusion that had infected Joseph Smith in Manchester, NY traveled six months later, 14 miles down the road to Hydesville, NY. There the Fox sisters began communicating with spirits of the dead. The epidemic continued and later on that year Andrew Jackson Davis published "Nature's Divine Revelations". Davis believed that the spirit in man continued on after death and moved on into any number of other worlds or spheres. He believed that the departed spirit would be in a state of consciousness or even in a higher state of consciousness. His book is still widely read and believed today.

The Fox sisters managed national attention as alleged spirits rapped out messages in a simple alphabet code to loved ones who traveled from all over the nation to communicate with recently departed loved ones. The Fox sisters did not use magic glasses or golden scrolls but the phenomenon expanded across the world and soon mediums were bringing messages everywhere. The Fox sisters later confessed that they had produced the rapping noises through simple chicanery, but the delusion epidemic could not be diminished by the truth.

I understand that the Psychic network has been removed from television. They apparently could not pay the bills. You would think that people who are gifted to know the future would have been able to foresee these financial difficulties. Mediums and psychics, those, who divine through tea leaves, palm readers and a host of others who allegedly tell fortunes permeate our civilization. Popular actors, actresses, musicians and authors influence our civilization and are themselves inspired by messages from dead spirits. At best, the messages are complete fabrications; the worst case-scenario is that demons are guiding and directing our society through mediums to the media using those with power to persuade.

Bahai Faith - 1850

Bahai Faith teaches the unity of all religions of mankind. It arose in 1850 in Iran from the teachings of Mirza Ali Mohammed and Mirza Hussein Ali. Both men were thought to be manifestations of God. The emphasis of the movement is service to others and its goals are universal peace, love, fellowship and equality. As idyllic and harmless as those principles appear to be, they were threatening to the Ayatollah Khomeini and when he came into power, the followers of Bahai Faith faced persecution.

The movement is currently directed by an elected order, which humbly refers to itself as The Universal House of Justice. The movement is popular among college students and flourishes on campuses. There are some four million adherents to the Bahai Faith.

Anglican Communion - 1867

Many religious movements are well known and wield a great influence. Others, although influential, are little known and still others are of little consequence and also generally unknown. The Anglican Communion certainly falls into the category of little known and of little consequence. However, they did come into existence during the time frame of the appearance of the other end time false messiahs.

The Anglican Communion comprises all of the churches worldwide, which are in communion with the Church of England. The first conference met in 1867 and continues to meet every ten years. It is not exactly a one World religion, but it is a small step in that direction.

Theosophy - 1875

We are listing these ideas and beliefs in chronological order. If we were combining them by subject matter we might want to list Theosophy along with Spiritism because many of the adherents to one advocate the other. The word Theosophy literally translates as "the wisdom of God". They believe that man has intuitive insight into the nature of God and that one can tap into this intuition through yoga and the wisdom of eastern religions. The first Theosophy society was founded in 1875.

Christian Science - 1879

The delusional disease that was so prevalent in the State of New York in 1867 moved in 1879 to Boston. There, Mary Baker Glover T. Patterson Eddy began the Christian Science movement, which was and continues to be neither. It is certainly not Christian and it is certainly not science.

The Christian Science Monitor is one of the most respected newspapers in publication. The paper is known for maintaining objectivity in reporting. The Monitor can be objective since the authors do not believe the material world truly exists.

According to them, only mental attitude exists and that in our minds we can be positive or negative in thinking. On the negative side there is Satan, sin, evil, sickness and death and on the positive side there is God, goodness, health and life, though none of these actually exist. They do not believe in mind over matter, as they believe in mind *only* and *no* matter. When a member of the Christian Science sect dies, he is encouraged towards positive thinking and should he refuse to come around they humor him and bury him.

Christian Science has a full-time healing ministry engaged in by people called practitioners. Curing of disease through prayer is regarded as a necessary element for salvation. Evening meetings may include the testimonial sharing of healing experiences by members of the denomination. Followers are not compelled by the church to use spiritual healing, but most members probably do. Many go to dentists and physicians who treat problems of the eye and for such procedures as setting bones or delivering babies.

Mrs. Eddy wrote "Science and Health with Key to the Scriptures," first issued in 1875 and repeatedly revised over the next 35 years. She believed herself to be the woman clothed with the sun in Revelation 12 and the Christian Science faith believes her writings are as authentic as Scriptures.

Christian Science congregations sponsor reading rooms for Bible study and "Science and Health" lessons. These sources are also the basis of worship services. Presently there are about 3,000 branches in 57 countries. Obviously the delusional disease is highly contagious. It just has to be the fleas.

Jehovah's Witnesses - 1879

The religious organization, known as Jehovah's Witnesses since 1931, was originally called the Russellites after its founder, Charles Taze Russell. Dr. McCorkle the former president of the old Philadelphia College of Bible used to affectionately refer to them as witnesses against Jehovah.

Russell, a native of Pittsburgh, renounced the teachings of Christian denominations because he could not accept what he saw as conflicting ideas of eternal damnation and a merciful God. Again we see the influence of surrounding philosophies in society influencing theology. Russell threw out the explicit instruction of God's word, because he could not reconcile it with his subjective conclusions. Among other impossible positions, Russell believed that the Holy name of God is Jehovah. That would be rather remarkable since there is no letter "J" in the Hebrew alphabet.

A local newspaper, The Brooklyn Eagle, once claimed in print that Russell was unschooled. Russell sued the paper for liable. In the ensuing court case it was proven that Russell was absolutely illiterate in both Greek and Hebrew.

This delusional disease has been running rampant in our land and has left people in a state where facts are of no consideration. By the late 1980s, the Witnesses had more than 3,700,000 members worldwide and were doing work in more than 200 countries and territories. The society has, over the years, distributed more than 4 billion copies of "The Watchtower" in 210 languages. Total distribution of its modern English Bible was more than 43 million by the early 1990s.

Local congregations are called Kingdom Halls. Members are expected to spend several hours a week at the halls in meetings and Bible study and as much time as possible in door-to-door preaching and distribution of Watch Tower literature. Each hall has a board of elders that elects a presiding minister for a one-year term. Only men are qualified to hold teaching or administrative positions in the society.

I have been to a Kingdom Hall, and I can testify that the place was a haven for demonic activity. Witnesses actually deny the deity of Jesus and have invented numerous fanciful and biblically impossible views especially in regards to prophecy. They dissociate themselves from all civil societies refusing to vote, run for public offices, serve in the armed forces, or take part in any patriotic exercises. This stand has frequently brought them in conflict with governments in many countries. During World War II, thousands of Witnesses were interned in Nazi concentration camps and they are still persecuted in some Eastern European nations.

Golden Dawn Society - 1887

According to the almanac the Golden Dawn Society was only one of the large number of occult organizations that flourished in the latter half of the 19th century. It was a strange and intellectual society founded in 1877 by three former Rosicrucians.[15] The group professed to have important secrets of occult knowledge and taught the precepts of white and black magic. The group attracted many very influential celebrities, scholars, authors and eccentrics. One well-known member Aleister Crowley was ultimately expelled from the society for practicing black magic.

Modernism - 1893

The same century that gave us magic glasses, golden tablets, the Fox sisters, Mary Baker Glover T. Patterson Eddy, Ellen White and Charles Tayes Russell, also gave us higher criticism and modernism. Higher criticism appeared on the same continent that gave us romanticism, rationalism, socialism and a renewed fervor for the *"ism"* that fondly unites them all is anti-Semitism.

Higher criticism subjects the Bible to literary examination as if it were the product of human authors. It denies the miraculous and supernatural authority of God's Word and is part of the mass exodus from absolutes into the oblivion of total subjectivity. It provides a pseudo scientific excuse to ignore God's word so that we can attempt to lean on our own understanding.

Today, pastors are being taught in seminaries that the Bible can *become* the Word of God if it speaks to you. Passages, which are hard to understand or hard to obey, are ignored. When the Scriptures prohibit homosexual behavior, it is understood to be a cultural prejudice. Insistence on sexual morality and marital fidelity are seen as antiquated concepts for another age.

The modernist wants to hold on to the resurrection but deny miracles, so they teach Jesus is raised in our hearts but not in the body. Where Nietzsche concluded that the Christian God is dead, modernism attempts to embalm the Christian church. They take out the guts, remove the life and decorate the body. The liberal church today is a decorated shell. It has lipstick and mascara, but has no life. The very Scriptures that they have denied predicted their existence. The Bible tells us that *"in the latter times some shall depart from the faith, giving heed to seducing spirits, and doctrines of devils;"* (1 Timothy 4:1) *"having a form of godliness, but denying the power thereof"* (2 Timothy 3:5).

Are We There Yet?

Pentecostalism - 1901

I desperately do not desire to offend or to alienate any of the dear saints and true brothers and sisters in the faith who consider themselves to be Pentecostal. Please stop the protest letters. Would you believe some of my best friends are Pentecostal? I did not select these topics arbitrarily. I did not select them at all. I only listed them from the "Ideas and Beliefs" section of "The Almanac".

From the time of Jesus until 1775 there were 36 new ideas or beliefs. In the next 140 years up to 1915 there were 39 new ideas and beliefs entering our world. That phenomenon needs to be addressed. Our civilization has been invaded, overwhelmed and conquered by these sundry *"isms"*. Each of them individually has impacted our society and collectively they have produced an end time world that is prepared to be governed by the antichrist where governments are without God, individuals are without guilt and above reproach, and there is no revelation from God; no absolutes.

According to "The Almanac," Pentecostalism is one of these end time movements, as is Capitalism. Most of the Christians I know are capitalists and many of the Christians I know are Pentecostal. That does not change the fact that both movements no matter how genuine or correct they may be are a part of the end time trend.

The origin of Pentecostalism appears to stem from Agnes Ozman, a student at a Bible college in Topeka, Kansas. At a religious meeting on New Years day 1901, she began speaking in tongues. From that single incident a movement spread across America, more prominently in rural areas. According to "The Almanac", "Pentecostal services are enthusiastic and rousing with strong emphasis on music and participation on the part of the congregation."[16]

The Pentecostal beliefs see tongues as an evidence of true conversion. The difficulty here is that both the aforementioned witnesses against Jehovah and Mormons use tongues in their services. Both deny the deity of Jesus yet speak in tongues. Jesus said, *"if ye believe not that I am [he], ye shall die in your sins."* (John 8:24)[17] In Romans 10:9 we read, *"That if thou shalt confess with thy mouth the Lord Jesus,*[18] *... thou shalt be saved* (Romans 10:9).

The stress on tongues has served to divide the true church and unites Christians with unbelieving cults and false religions. When the Devil sits in the Temple posing as God, he will be worshipped as God and the one world religious system will probably worship him with ecstatic utterances expressed in unknown tongues.

The Pentecostal faith also tends to emphasize experience over doctrine. A miracle will validate a believer more than testimony and prophecy will take precedent over exegesis. This trend contributes to the society-wide movement away from the absolute authority of the Scriptures. We are living in an age that looks very much like the perilous times described in 2 Timothy 3:2-5 where we read, *"For men shall be lovers of their own selves, covetous, boasters, proud, blasphemers, disobedient to parents, unthankful, unholy, without natural affection, trucebreakers, false accusers, incontinent, fierce, despisers of those that are good, traitors, heady, highminded, lovers of pleasures more than lovers of God; Having a form of godliness, but denying the power thereof: from such turn away."* 2 Timothy 3:2-5.

Conclusion

From Romanticism to Vitalism we can see moral absolutes giving way to situation ethics. The convictions of a divinely placed conscience are replaced by individualistic boasts of self-virtue. False priests have ameliorated the human conscience by blaming parents, governments, genetics and stimuli for our decisions. They leave the individual above reproach. These priests will not hear or encourage our confession, nor commend to us the need for sacrifice. Rather, they have provided us with phony alibis and false excuses.

From the Illuminati to the Nazis we see the influence of the theory of evolution being applied to governments without God. Each political theory attempts to bring in its own version of utopia. On one side we see a rise of Nationalism, moving from Capitalism through Fascism and Nazism and influenced by Nihilism. On the other extreme we see Socialism and Communism influenced by Marxism and Trotskyism. Both resulted in cruel and failed dictators who had no respect for human rights or life. They were frustrated by attempting to govern without prayer and without council from the living God and in their frustration they turned to anti-Semitism. The Jews were and are slaughtered from the left in the East. The Jews were and are slaughtered from the right in the West. And under the dominion of the antichrist, the Jews will be slaughtered universally.

The antichrist will establish a one world religious system. That final false church is referred to as a great whore in Revelation 17:1 and is pictured as a woman who is unfaithful to the one to whom she was designed to be true.

In Genesis the first woman was created to be the complement of one man. Later God used the woman to picture a religious system of His creation and answering to His call. Judaism is that religion throughout the Old Testament and Jehovah calls Israel His wife. In the New Testament it is the church and it is likened to the bride of Christ. In the Book of Revelation four women appear representing religion.

In chapter 12 we see the woman clothed with the sun, representing Israel. In chapter 19 we see the bride of Christ representing the true church. In chapter 2 we are introduced to Jezebel who represents the paganism of the past and in the great whore we see the picture of the false church of the future.

The language of Revelation describes this future church for us. In 17:1 she is called *"great,"* which refers to the influence, power and position of the church. She is depicted as sitting upon many waters. In verse 15 the waters are interpreted as referring to *"peoples and multitudes and nations and tongues,"* showing that her great influence will be universal.

There are additional references to this universal influence. In verses 3 and 7 she sits on a scarlet colored beast. The beast is the end time world ruler and the end time church is pictured as riding upon the beast. The one who is riding is in control. In the beginning stages, the church controls the beast. In verse 5 the church is called *"Babylon the great,"* showing that the chief concerns of the end time church are purely earthly and temporal.

Jude 4 mentions the creeps as existing in the church at the time of that writing. We see creeps again in 2 Timothy 3:6 in the context of the perilous times of the last days. From the beginning of the Church wolves have entered in disguised in the clothing of sheep as Jesus taught in Matthew 7:15. In the first epistle of John the spirit of antichrist is already at work and is the spirit that shall also come in the future (1 John 4:3). In Matthew 13 Jesus teaches us a parable about the wheat and the tares.

From the very beginning we see the wicked one sneaking in and sowing tares alongside of the wheat. In 1 John we are told that many antichrists had already come at the time of that writing (1 John 2:18). John writes that the spirit of antichrist is already at work in the world (1 John 4:3).

When John sees these antichrists appearing, he recognizes that he is living in the last days. The church age is the last days and we are in the last days of the church age. Throughout the church age there have been false teachers that have crept in with stealth and taught heresy. John called these false teachers antichrists and Jesus referred to them as false messiahs and prophesied to His disciples that the appearance of these false teachers in large numbers is a sign of His coming.

From Unitarianism to Pentecostalism we see many false messiahs arising and teaching the bogus doctrines predicted in the Scriptures. These sundry isms are preparing the world religions to join into and become the great harlot of Revelation. They have been carrying on their surreptitious activity within and against the true Church throughout this entire age and the appearance of them in mass is a sign of the Lord's return.

World War

> *"For nation shall rise against nation, and kingdom against kingdom"* Matthew 24:7

> *"And I will set the Egyptians against the Egyptians: and they shall fight every one against his brother, and every one against his neighbour; city against city, [and] kingdom against kingdom."* Isaiah 19:2

> *"And nation was destroyed of nation, and city of city: for God did vex them with all adversity."* 2 Chronicles 15:6

The phrase *"nation against nation and kingdom against kingdom"* is an idiom in the Hebrew language. In 2 Chronicles 15, the phrase is a product of the vexation from God. In the preceding verse, the great vexations from God were upon all the inhabitants of the countries. The vexation was complete and expansive and extended to the very ends of the earth. The idiom *"nation against nation"* refers to extending to the end of the barriers of the area being discussed. In Isaiah 19 the area being discussed is Egypt. We read about a civil war erupting in that land. The phrase *"kingdom against kingdom"* tells us that the civil war will involve the entire nation of Egypt extending to the end of the barriers of that land.

The context of Matthew 24 is the world. In verse 9 we see that the Jewish believers of that age *"will be hated by all nations"*. In verse 14 we see how the *"gospel of the kingdom will be preached in all the world for a witness unto all nation."*. Since the context is the world, the idiom *"nation against nation and kingdom against kingdom"* would refer to a worldwide conflict that would extend to the ends of the earth. No conflict like that ever occurred before 1917. We called the conflict World War I and the sequel, World War II, quickly followed. This universal conflict is mentioned in the Talmud[19] in reference to the Messiah.

"If you shall see kingdom rising against each other in turn then give heed to the footsteps of the Messiah." Beresheit Rabbah 42:4

This concept is also mentioned in the Zohar.[20] My guess is that the Jewish sources are quoting the words of Jesus. The close connection between the followers of Jesus and the Pharisees is attested to in the Babylonian Talmud.[21] They both continued in the Synagogue and they lived, worked and worshipped together until the second Jewish revolt. At that time the leading rabbi, Akiba, declared Bar Kochba to be the Messiah. The Jewish believers in Jesus saw Akiba as the false prophet of Revelation chapter 13 and they saw Bar Kochba as the antichrist. The Jewish believers refused to assist their Jewish brothers in the revolt against Rome. The Roman Empire put the Jewish revolt down decisively. Jerusalem was made into a Gentile city, the Jewish people were dispersed from the land and the Diaspora began. Jewish people who believed in Jesus were blamed because of the lack of support. At this point, Christianity and Judaism became divided by bitterness.

However, before the division, when they were growing up together, the things that Jesus taught found there way into Judaism and they have left an evidential mark in the writings of the rabbis. Jesus taught that before He returns there will be many false, deceiving messiahs.

From the time Jesus spoke we saw nothing for 1,740 years, then we saw an uncanny eruption of new ideas and beliefs enter and influence our culture from 1772 to 1915. Also, Jesus taught that there would be a worldwide conflict prior to His return. The rabbis recognized the significance of these things Jesus taught, and they wrote about this worldwide conflict as corresponding with the coming of the Messiah. Just two years after the last of the false messiahs, World War

Are We There Yet?

I began and just three years after the completion of World War II the nation of Israel was reborn.

Famines and Earthquakes

After speaking about the wars, Jesus said there would be famines in diverse places. Then he mentioned earthquakes. The King James Bible mentions pestilence in Matthew 24:7.

One of our missionaries often asks, "Do you have to read a King James Bible to be saved?" and then he winsomely supplies the answer with, "Maybe Not! But, why take the chance." I prefer the literalness of the King James Bible. Some translations stress clarity in English and sacrifice fidelity to the Greek and Hebrew texts. I prefer a hard to comprehend truth to an easily understood lie. However, a translation preference has nothing to do with the textual discussion.[22] Newer translations have the benefit of more recent archaeological evidence. The more documents we find, the closer we are to determining what the autographs[23] must have been like.

Those who write and preach on prophecy, for the most part, ignore the word famine and go directly to the earthquakes. I suppose the new rule of hermeneutics[24] is the principle of alphabetical order. E is for earthquakes and F is for famines and since E comes first in the alphabet we can go bonkers over earthquakes and ignore the famine reference entirely.

When I began this project, I thought that I was not scholarly enough to produce a book on prophecy. After reading the books that have already been written and listening to the messages of the most popular speakers on the subject of Bible prophecy, I have come to the conclusion that lack of scholarship is a pre-requisite for acceptance in the field. I am probably over qualified.

Similarities between the description of the tribulation in Revelation 6 and Matthew's record of the Olivet Discourse are undeniable. The first seal describes the end time ruler entering on a white horse; then we see him taking peace from the earth in the second seal. In the third seal we see a famine, which is not an unusual consequence of the first two seals. Following the famine we see pestilence, which is not an unusual result of the famine. In the sixth seal we read about a great earthquake. These events are not natural progressions but are supernatural signs. These signs identify Jesus with the traditional rabbinical writings of the Messiah and the messianic times.

Jesus calls the appearance of famines and earthquakes *"the beginning of sorrows"*.[25] There were possibly eleven historical famines in the Scriptures.[26] The first occurs in Genesis 12:10. As a result of this famine Abraham journeyed into Egypt. It is in Egypt that Abraham acquired a handmaid for Sarah, named Hagar. Hagar later became the mother of Ishmael and as such became the mother of the Arab people.

The second famine in the Scriptures was in Genesis 26. Because of this famine Isaac started to journey to Egypt, but in obedience to a warning from the Lord, Isaac stopped in the land of Gerar.

The next famine mentioned is in the context of the interpretation of Pharaoh's dream by Joseph in Genesis 41. As a result of this famine, the family of Jacob ended up in Egyptian bondage for four hundred years. The first three famines in the Scriptures had to do with the lands of Egypt and Israel. The modern state of Israel became a nation in 1948 and Egypt has been a constituted state since 1971.

The fourth famine mentioned in Scripture is in the book of Ruth. This famine is significant because through it Ruth is introduced into the Jewish faith. As a result of this famine Ruth becomes one of the four women who are recorded in the genealogy of the Messiah (Matthew 1:5).

The next famine occurs in 2 Samuel 21. When Joshua led the children of Israel into Canaan land he was tricked into making an oath with the Gibeonites. King Saul broke that oath and the Lord brought a famine into the land of Judah. When King David saw the famine continue for three years, he knew it was not a coincidence or an arbitrary act of Mother Nature, but it was part of the disciplinary action of Father God. David took the necessary action to make atonement with the offended Gibeonites and the three-year famine was removed.

The sixth famine occurred in the land of Samaria during the days of Elijah (1 Kings 18:2)[27] and is the background for a confrontation between the most wicked of the Kings of Israel and the greatest prophet. The incidents of this famine are used to identify Elijah as one of the witnesses in Revelation 11. He had the power to shut up the heavens (James 5:1)

The Lord also used famines to authenticate Elisha's ministry. There is a famine in 2 Kings 4:38 and another mentioned in 2 Kings 6:25. We number them as famines seven and eight, although they could be one and the same. In 2 Kings 8:1, Elisha predicts the ninth famine and it will last seven years in the Northern Kingdom. The tenth famine is mentioned in 2 Kings 25:3 and it coincides with the southern kingdom being taken into Babylonian captivity. Jeremiah makes mention of this famine in Chapter 14.

The eleventh and final famine is mentioned in Nehemiah 5:3 after the return from Babylonian captivity. Although the language of Nehemiah is such that you get the idea that the famine was not all that grievous, but rather, the Jewish people were on the whiny side, if you can believe such a thing.

In commentary on the first Biblical famine at the time of Abraham, the Midrash[28] on Genesis says that there is only one famine that reappears at different times and then there will be one famine at the time of the Messiah. Famines occurred in the history of the land of Israel to confirm Patriarchs, Prophets and Kings. The future famines will confirm the times of the Messiah. By referring to famines as a sign of His coming, Jesus is clarifying to the disciples that He is the promised Messiah.

Next, Jesus mentioned earthquakes. It is on this topic that writers and preachers in the area of Bible prophesy pave new ground in lunacy. I tried to join in myself and came at the truth through a back door. The prophecy books I had been consulting had been telling me that there is an uncanny increase in both the frequency and the intensity of earthquakes in these, the last days. They all agreed on this concept and had conjured up evidence to support it. After searching through the statistics, the only increase that I could discover was the growing lack of integrity amongst the Christian leaders who teach and write on prophetic themes. They mistakenly see the increase of earthquakes as an indicator that the return of Jesus must be near. This popular concept is wrong on two counts. Not only are earthquakes not increasing, but also the Bible never indicated that they would. When Jesus spoke of earthquakes He never predicted an increase, but rather He directed us to focus on the biblical concept of the earthquake phenomenon.

Earthquakes, like other cataclysmic events in the Scriptures often demonstrate God's presence and power. Throughout the Old Testament we see earthquakes as manifestations of God's wrath and judgment (1 Samuel 14:15; Psalms 18:7,8; Isaiah 5:25; 13:13; 29:6; Joel 3:16; Amos 1:1,2; 8:7,8; Micah 1:3-7; Nahum 1:5,6; Haggai 2:6, 21). In the New Testament when the Messiah was being sacrificed on the tree, the earth shook (Matthew 27:51) and it was no human being that rolled away the stone that sealed Jesus into the tomb. It was a great earthquake (Matthew 28:2). When the New Testament church prayed, the place where they gathered together was shaken and the Spirit's presence was exhibited (Acts 4:31). Paul and Silas were freed when God's presence was manifested in an earthquake (Acts 16:26).

In Exodus 19:18, when the Lord met with Moses to give the Ten Commandments, we see that the *"whole mount quaked greatly"*. In Hebrews 12:26, the author equates that earthquake with the final shaking of heaven and earth that takes place at the end of the tribulation. In the tribulation we see an earthquake predicted at the end of the sixth seal and another one predicted for the end of the seventh seal.

In Revelation chapter 8 two more earthquakes are mentioned, one just before the seventh trumpet and another just after it. That earthquake which is mentioned at the end of the seventh trumpet might be the same one referred to in Revelation 16:18 as the greatest ever on earth. It splits Jerusalem into three parts and could be the same earthquake that is predicted in Zechariah 14. The Mount of Olives is split and a spectacular escape route is formed, allowing the Jewish people to flee from the siege of the antichrist at the conclusion of the Armageddon campaign. Zechariah 14 introduces these events with the phrase *"the day of the Lord"*.

The expression *"day of the Lord"* occurs some 30 times in the Scriptures.[29] Earthquakes are frequently associated with the wrath of God in that day. The first time we are introduced to the day of the Lord is in Isaiah 2:12 and in 21 we read, *"he ariseth to shake terribly the earth"*. (Isaiah 2:21)

The next references to that day are in Isaiah 13:6 and 9 and in verse 13 we read, *"Therefore I will shake the heavens, and the earth shall remove out of her place, in the wrath of the LORD of hosts, and in the day of his fierce anger."*

The book of Joel mentions the day of the Lord 5 times; Joel 1:15, 2:1, 2:11, 2:31, 3:14, and the earthquake that is associated with that day is described in 2:10,

> *"The earth shall quake before them; the heavens shall tremble: the sun and the moon shall be dark, and the stars shall withdraw their shining."* Joel 2:10

All the other earthquakes that are predicted in the Scriptures seem to be associated with the land of Israel. During the awesome shakedown of heaven and earth, *"the LORD will have mercy on Jacob"* (Isaiah 14:1). When Israel is attacked by the multi national Islamic confederation united under Gog, the invaders are defeated by the decree of the Lord, through an earthquake and cosmic hailstones (Ezekiel 38:17-23). The shaking is going to take place in the land of Israel but the reference is not just to a geographical location. The prediction of Ezekiel 38 clearly includes the fact that the people of Israel are to be returned to the land.

> Ezekiel 38:8 *"After many days thou shalt be visited: in the latter years thou shalt come into the land [that is] brought back from the sword, [and is] gathered out of many people, against the mountains of Israel, which have been always waste: but it is brought forth out of the nations, and they shall dwell safely all of them."*

The earthquake in Zechariah 14 that we mentioned above also takes place in the land of Israel. These earthquakes could not have occurred before 1948, the year that the modern nation of Israel was established. According to Zechariah 14, the escape that the end time earthquake provides allows the Jewish people to flee to the same place that they fled to at the incident of a previous earthquake that took place at the time of Uzziah the king of Judah. This earthquake left considerable damage in the Middle East.

At Tel Sheva, which is most likely the location of Biblical Beer Sheva, there is evidence of an earthquake that partially destroyed level three, which would coincide with the time of Uzziah's rule.[30] Excavations at Tel Lachish seem to indicate that the same earthquake caused devastation to that city as well. There is also archaeological evidence for this earthquake at many different locations including Hazor.

At Hazor there were indications of the idolatry which was forbidden by the prophet Isaiah, who warned how the Lord will remove the idols by shaking the earth (Isaiah 2:19-21). We know the time of this earthquake from Josephus who tells us it occurred on the Day of Atonement in the year that Uzziah was struck with leprosy.[31] Amos predicted this earthquake two years before it occurred. It was a warning to the nation of Israel to abandon their idolatrous ways and turn to the Lord. This final devastating and extensive earthquake was the last chance for the Northern Kingdom, the Kingdom of Israel, to repent before she was dispersed among the nations.

The next Biblical earthquake is in Ezekiel 38 and follows the return of that same nation of Israel to her rightful place. By mentioning earthquakes, the Messiah is telling us that one of the signs of His return is the restoration of the idolatrous nation. The earthquakes that once were an indication of God's wrath and judgment upon his ancient people, now will be earthquakes of protection against their enemies and the means of providing a way of escape.

The first of the false messiahs appeared in 1752. According to the Almanac, the era of false messiahs lasts until 1915. After the accounts of false messiahs, we are told of worldwide conflicts. The first of these conflicts began in 1917, just two years after the last of the false messiahs. World War II ended in 1945, just three years before the establishment of the modern nation of Israel, which was restored in 1948.

The restored nation of Israel will be protected from an Islamic invasion by means of an earthquake before the tribulation. At the end of the tribulation another earthquake will be used to provide a way of escape from the final siege upon the city of Jerusalem, when the Messiah splits the Mount of Olives. The earthquakes that are predicted in Scripture all occur after Israel is restored as a nation. The references to earthquakes and famines clearly identify Jesus as Israel's Messiah and picture the messianic age.

Israel and Jerusalem

The famines and earthquakes mentioned in the Scriptures deal directly with the land of Israel and the city of Jerusalem. Jewish tradition sees them as a sign of the Messiah. When Jesus refers to famines and earthquakes He is both inferring that Israel will be a nation and He is declaring Himself to be Israel's Messiah. The signs of

Matthew 24 began in 1752 and take us up to the establishment of Israel in 1948. We're getting closer!

> *"When ye therefore shall see the abomination of desolation spoken of by Daniel the prophet, stand in the holy place,"* Matthew 24:15

The mention of the holy place takes us past 1948 up to the end of the Six-Day War in 1967 when the old city of Jerusalem was conquered by the Israeli army on June 7. Today we take the establishment of the nation of Israel for granted. We no longer realize that the modern nation of Israel is a fulfillment of prophecy. Israel has been a nation for over fifty years and in that time we have lost the enthusiasm for the miracle of that restored nation.

I am certain that before 1948 the dispensational[32] theologians were ridiculed for believing that the prophecies regarding the land of Israel were to be understood in a literal manner.

I am certain because my Presbyterian friends (an oxymoron) badger me today for holding on to a literal method of interpreting Bible prophecy. I realize that a nation being reborn is an amazing thing. Before it happened the cautious, logical and reasoned theologian could not fathom anything quite that spectacular. But the whole concept of prophecy is sensational.

The rapture with the sound of trumpets, the archangel's voice and the rising dead is all spectacular and difficult to imagine. The events of the tribulation, with the supernatural signs in the sky, the concept of a kingdom, the glimpse we get of the eternal state, a new heaven and a new earth are all events that are difficult to imagine as being true. Our limited, finite experience does not allow our minds to picture what these events might be like when fulfilled. It is only natural to shrink away from a literal interpretation to a more comfortable spiritual picture that we can comprehend and control. However, as amazing as the concept of restoration of the nation of Israel may be, it happened! Israel is back in the land and Jerusalem is a fact of history.

Are We There Yet?

In Isaiah 11:11 we read how the Lord will recover Israel a second time. The first time would have been from the Babylonian captivity. Not only do the Scriptures predict the return of the Jews, but also it is possible that the Scriptures predict the exact year for the return of both and perhaps even the exact day.

> " This [shall be] a sign to the house of Israel. Lie thou also upon thy left side, and lay the iniquity of the house of Israel upon it: [according] to the number of the days that thou shalt lie upon it thou shalt bear their iniquity. For I have laid upon thee the years of their iniquity, according to the number of the days, three hundred and ninety days: so shalt thou bear the iniquity of the house of Israel. And when thou hast accomplished them, lie again on thy right side, and thou shalt bear the iniquity of the house of Judah forty days: I have appointed thee each day for a year." Ezekiel 4:3b-6

The nation of Israel is given a sign; Ezekiel was to lie on his left side for three hundred and ninety days, one day for every year, for the iniquity of Israel. Then Ezekiel was instructed to bear the iniquity of the house of Judah forty days, one day for each year.

A sign is something visible and discernable. The application for the two periods of time is a mystery. Ezekiel is written from Babylon between 622 and 600 B.C. From the writing of Ezekiel forward there does not appear to be a place to apply the two periods of time designated for Israel and Judah. This sign by itself is not apparently recognizable. Combining the two terms we arrive at a total of four hundred and thirty years. That number does not help us much either. However, we can get some help from another passage of Scripture.

In Leviticus 26:1-13, the Lord reveals from Mount Sinai the plan of blessing for the Jewish people if they obey His commandments and walk in His statutes (Leviticus 26:3). In verses 14-31 we read about the severe judgments that Israel will endure if they fail to keep the covenant that they made with the Lord. These judgments will occur in succeeding phases, each increasing in intensity from the last. At the conclusion of each phase, the Jewish people are given an opportunity to repent. If they fail to repent, the Lord brings them into the next phase of discipline.

In verses 32-35 Israel arrives at the final stage of discipline, the Babylonian captivity. We can be certain that the Babylonian captivity is in view because the Scriptures refer to the land enjoying her Sabbath rest.[33]

In verses 36-39 the Scriptures leap past the Babylonian captivity and begin to describe the holocaust. The enemy nations are in these final verses as plural nations and the singular nation of Babylon is no longer in view. In verses 40-46 the Jewish people are promised a final and ultimate restoration, which will come in response to their national confession.

"...I will punish you seven times more for your sins." Leviticus 26:18

"...and will punish you yet seven times for your sins." Leviticus 26:24

"...I will chastise you seven times for your sins." Leviticus 26:28

Three times we read the phrase *"seven times more."* If we combine the sign of Ezekiel chapter 4 with the explanation of Leviticus 26, we can begin to see a possible solution. In Ezekiel, we were left with a total of four hundred and thirty years. From Leviticus we pick up two pieces of information. 70 years of punishment was accomplished in the Babylonian captivity. Which leaves us with 360 years. Then Leviticus tells us to multiply that number times 7. Which leaves us with 2520 years of punishment for the nation of Israel and for the house of Judah.

In the Summer of 606 B.C., Nebuchadnezzar entered into Israel and began the servitude of the nation which lasted until the Summer of 537 B.C. From the return of the Jewish people in 537 B.C., we need to move forward in time 2520 lunar years which converts in our solar calendar to 2483 years, 9 months and 21 days.

Are We There Yet?

2483 years 9 months and 21 days forward from 537 B.C., we arrive at the year 1948.[34] Counting back from May 14th, the birthday of Israel, we arrive at the date July 23, 537 B.C.

We do not know the day, but we do know the year and since Israel became a nation on the 14th of May, 1948 why would we not assume that the seventy years of Babylonian captivity ended on July 23, in the year 537 B.C.?

There is yet another application for the calculations of the 2483 years 9 months and 21 days. The third siege of Nebuchadnezzar was in 587 B.C., which began the Jerusalem desolation, which also was to last 70 years (Daniel 9:12). The conclusion of the 70 years of the *"desolations of Jerusalem"* occurred in the year 518 B.C.

Using the same calibrations as above, we add the 2483 years 9 months and 21 days and arrive at the year 1967. If August 16 was the day when the desolation of Jerusalem officially ended, then the fulfillment of the sign acted out by the prophet Ezekiel would be June 7 of the year 1967; the day and year of the restoration of the Old City of Jerusalem.

Now I know that we had to work backward to arrive at the starting days, but the starting years were historically accurate. Also, I realize that there would be little reason to combine Ezekiel 4 with Leviticus 26. However, it is a fact that the arithmetic of the years does total up to the time of the events in the history of modern Israel.

I admire the faith that would believe these facts to be only a coincidence. God predicted the restoration of the land and since he controls the events of time, you might expect the prophecy to be pretty close to the exact date.

CHAPTER FOUR

Seven Prophetic P's

I stole this message from so many good sources I cannot even begin to give the proper credit. The seven P's is an overview of prophetic and historic texts, which will unveil the reason for the great tribulation and the universal persecution of the Jewish people.

The Promise

When I was growing up, my parents frequently spoke about the coming of the Messiah. Unfortunately, it was not in realistic terms. If I would ask for my own car the answer would be "when the Messiah comes". My own room, a raise in my allowance, my own TV, my own phone or you name it, the Messiah would supply it. Of course it was not long before one realized the Messiah was not coming and the wish list would remain just that, a list of wishes. The coming of the Messiah has always been like that for the Jewish people - a wish list, not to be genuinely believed.

When Messiah Jesus did present himself as the sacrifice for the sins of the nation, the Jewish people were hoping for a very different scenario. Those who did believe in the genuine Messiah did so on the authority of the prophetic Scriptures. Admittedly, those scriptures would be difficult to interpret accurately. In Isaiah 11:10 we read about the glorious rest that will be enjoyed when the root of Jesse, the Messiah, takes his stand. However, 11:11 continues to describe the second gathering together. of the Lord's people and 11:12 clearly shows the gathering to be a universal one, from the four-corners of the earth.

Since the Jewish people were living in the land when Jesus came the first time, they would have had no idea how they were to understand this second gathering. It is obvious to us that the Messiah was scheduled to arrive on two different occasions. The Jewish people did not understand that and expected the Messiah to fulfill all the promises of both advents at the first arrival, which was the only arrival in their understanding.

Psalm 72 is just one of the many passages which describe the promised Messiah that the Jewish people were expecting. In 72:4 we see how the salvation they were anticipating was economic and not spiritual.

> *"He shall judge the poor of the people, he shall save the children of the needy, and shall break in pieces the oppressor."* Psalms 72:4

Along with economic deliverance, the Psalm makes military and political promises. In verse 9, his enemies will lick the dust. In verse 11, we read that all nations will serve him. In 72:7, the peace that He brings is promised to last as long as the moon endures. A kingdom is clearly promised to coincide with the arrival of the Messiah king. That kingdom is one of judgment and justice (Psalm 72:2). The kingdom includes prosperity in verses 6-7. The question is, what happened to this promised kingdom?

The Presentation

In Matthew 12 there was a man brought to Jesus who was possessed by a devil[1]. Before this man was brought to Him, Jesus had healed a man of a withered hand on the Sabbath. As a result, the

Pharisees conspired together on how they might bring down the ministry of Jesus.

> "*<u>Then</u> the Pharisees went out and held a council against him, how they might destroy him.*" Matthew 12:14

I cannot imagine that the Pharisees intended to kill Jesus. I think it is far more likely that the Pharisees were plotting how they might bring the ministry and the reputation of Jesus to naught. In 12:15-16, the passage continues to describe how Jesus knew the heart of the Pharisees and chose not to provoke them further. Jesus instructed everyone to "*not make him known*". In 12:17-21, Jesus quotes Isaiah 42:1-4 and in doing so identifies Himself as the promised Messiah. "<u>*Then*</u> *was brought unto him one possessed with a devil.*" I think the use of the word "*then*" connects Matthew 12:14 and 22. The man brought to Jesus was the result of the council to destroy His ministry.

Jesus had claimed to be the Messiah, but the Pharisees were certain that His claim was a false one. They intended to expose Him as a phony and they brought this demonized man before Jesus so that He might be publicly exposed as a fraud.

In order to perform an exorcism, one must first ascertain the demon's name, then the demon is exorcised with some kind of spiritual power of attorney. He is commanded to leave by name and by the authority of a higher name. We use the highest name of Jesus whereas the Rabbis of Jesus day almost certainly used the name YHVH. However, one must first discover the name of the demon. Now, this demonized man was dumb so that he could not speak the name of the demon: He was also blind so he could not write down the demon's name. Only the true Messiah could cast out such a demon so the Pharisees were certain that Jesus would fail.

These were messianic times. The prophecy of Daniel's seventy weeks made it clear that the Messiah was soon to come. There were certainly many false claimants roaming around the countryside. These self- anointed ones were probably preaching, teaching and gathering expectant crowds. They probably enjoyed a lot of attention, a lot of good hospitality and a lot of free meals. They would have drawn crowds and interest away from the Pharisees.

The Pharisees could and probably did use this poor, wretched, demonized man as a false Messiah test kit to expose them. When the pretender to David's throne was incapable of healing the man, the Pharisees could then announce to the crowds that the regular weekly Bible study meets on Tuesday night.

> "*<u>Then</u> was brought unto him one possessed with a devil, blind, and dumb: and he healed him, insomuch that the blind and dumb both spake and saw. And all the people were amazed, and said, 'Is not this the son of David?'*" Matthew 12:22-23

The well-meaning Pharisees thought they were performing a public service. They had no idea how significant that public service truly was. Instead of exposing another false messiah, they ended up revealing the genuine character of the true and only Messiah.

When Jesus healed the man, He proved that He was indeed the promised seed of David. The Pharisees unwittingly authenticated His ministry. The crowd responded appropriately, "*Is not this the son of David?*"[2] They were looking for the Pharisees to recognize and confirm the glorious truth. The Pharisees could not deny the miracle and this demonized man was changed in a supernatural manner, so instead, they said that is was done by the power of the adversary and not by the power of God. Jesus, in response made the most dynamic declaration.

> "*But if I cast out devils by the Spirit of God, <u>then</u> the kingdom of God is come unto you*" Matthew 12:28

There is no doubt about it. The words are written in red. The Lord Himself clarified with certainty that the promised kingdom was at this point in time presented to the Jewish people.

The Postponement

I apologize for using the term postponement. God is sovereign. He makes no mistakes in His plans, and He never has to readjust His thinking. Years ago, after I preached on this subject, a woman objected to the term and suggested a more suitable word. Her word was consistent with the alliteration. I remember thinking how perfect her suggestion was. Unfortunately, that is all I remember. I have thoroughly searched through the thesaurus to no avail so we are stuck with the word postponement. The kingdom was promised and presented, then something happened. Israel commits what is commonly called the "unpardonable sin" (Matthew 12:31-32[3]).

Since Jesus has propitiated or satisfied all that the justice of God demanded, there would be no such sin which we can perform for which the sacrifice of Jesus has not provided forgiveness. In John 6:47 Jesus promised eternal life belongs to all those who believe in Him, and from John 3:36 we know that all those who believe not are already condemned. Unbelief would not be the unpardonable sin, because we all were unbelievers first and we have come to faith and have been forgiven.

I think Jesus was speaking specifically of Israel's national rejection of Him. This sin will not be forgiven in the age when Jesus was speaking, nor in the next age. However, there is an age when this sin will be forgiven. *"Then answered all the people, and said, His blood [be] on us, and on our children."* (Matthew 27:25)

The next age is the age of the church, which began at the day of Pentecost and continues until the rapture, which closes out the church age. Anytime after that the nation of Israel can be forgiven.

In Matthew 12:22, Jesus performed a sign miracle to show His credentials as the promised Messiah. The Pharisees rejected the clear evidence and in 12:38, they had the audacity to ask for a sign. Jesus told them that the only sign that would be given them now, was the sign of the prophet Jonah.

That sign looks to the resurrection, which precludes the fact of the crucifixion, which is a product of the national rejection of the kingdom presentation. The Jewish people asked for a sign. Jesus said, *"an evil and adulterous generation[4] seeketh after a sign"*.

From this incident forward, Jesus calls the Jewish people a wicked and adulterous generation (Matthew 12:45 and Matthew 16:4). In Matthew 23 Jesus pronounced eight woes upon the Pharisees who rejected Him. He called them hypocrites repeatedly in this section and referred to them as blind guides and fools. In 23:34-36 He pronounced that the generation that rejected Him was responsible for all the righteous blood that was shed from Genesis to 2 Chronicles; the entire Jewish Scriptures.

In this very unusual instance the meek and lowly Jesus declared His true worth. The evil generation that had rejected the precious son of the highest had been set aside and the Kingdom that was both promised and presented now was set aside. In Matthew 23:37-39 we read how the nation will not see their King again until they acknowledge the true identity of the one they had rejected.

The Proclamation

"O Jerusalem, Jerusalem, [thou] that killest the prophets, and stonest them which are sent unto thee, how often would I have gathered thy children together, even as a hen gathereth her chickens under [her] wings, and ye would not! Behold, your house is left unto you desolate. For I say unto you, Ye shall not see me henceforth, till ye shall say, Blessed [is] he that cometh in the name of the Lord." Matthew 23:39

We refer to this statement of Jesus as The Proclamation. This statement provides the motivation for the universal, satanic hatred of the Jewish people. Satan is the prince of the power of the air (Ephesians 2:2) and the god of this world (2 Corinthians 4:4). He is the one who will be dethroned when the King and the kingdom are restored. Jesus established a pre-requisite for the establishment of the kingdom, which is the national confession of the Jewish people.

To prevent the King from returning, Satan must prevent the Jewish confession. Dead Jews cannot confess, so the adversary has at every juncture established policies of anti-Semitism in every nation. The universal hatred of the Jewish people is otherwise an inexplicable phenomenon, but this phenomenon proves the existence of God, the veracity of the Word and validates the faith of us who recognize the dispensations in the Scriptures.

In that great proclamation we see the phrase, *"Blessed is he that cometh in the name of the Lord"*.[5] The phrase comes from the Psalms and has become part of the Jewish wedding ceremony.

In the traditional Jewish wedding the bride waits for the groom, after the wedding he does all the waiting. In the Jewish wedding the groom assumes the role of God[6]. In that role the groom is the celebrity of the wedding. The bride and her party wait with the rabbi for the groom and his entourage to assemble. They congregate in another hall in the same building or sometimes in an entirely different location. The wait can be an hour or more. When the groom's party is fully assembled they put him on a chair, place the chair on their shoulders and carry him in with instruments and singing. When the rabbi hears the music he knows the wedding party is approaching. He alerts the bride and her family and announces the groom's arrival by shouting the Hebrew phrase "Baruch Haba Bashem Adonoi". By using this phrase Jesus pictures the nation of Israel recognizing Him and its relationship to Him.

The Persecution

"Then shall they deliver you up to be afflicted, and shall kill you: and ye shall be hated of all nations for my name's sake." Matthew 24:9

The persecution that Jesus predicts is universal. If any Jewish people are left alive, they could confess the Nation's iniquity, the Messiah would be able to return and Satan would be dethroned. If Satan is going to keep his dominion, every Jew must be killed. In order to be certain that all the Jews have been slaughtered, the world has to be conquered. Hitler attempted to extinguish all the Jews and to conquer the World simultaneously. The next guy will acquire World dominion first and then annihilate the Jews at his leisure.

The steps to World dominion could begin with the prophecy of Isaiah 17. We read there about the ultimate destruction of the city of Damascus. The majority of the commentaries see this passage as referring to the devastation of Syria as a result of the Assyrian invasion. However, the passage begins with the phrase *"The burden of Damascus..."*. Isaiah seems to use the term *"burden of"* to introduce texts that include references to end time events.[7]

> *"In that day shall his strong cities be as a forsaken bough, and an uppermost branch, which they left because of the children of Israel: and there shall be desolation.* Isaiah 17:9

The expression *"in that day"* is also a phrase that has end time reference. It seems that the children of Israel are mentioned as being the cause of the ruin of Damascus and not the nation of Assyria.

> *"Woe to the multitude of many people, [which] make a noise like the noise of the seas; and to the rushing of nations..."* Isaiah 17:12

17:12 refers to an invasion upon the nation of Israel by many nations following the destruction of Damascus at the hands of the Jews.

> *"The nations shall rush like the rushing of many waters: but [God] shall rebuke them, and they shall flee far off, and shall be chased as the chaff of the mountains before the wind, and like a rolling thing before the whirlwind. And behold at eveningtide trouble; [and] before the morning he [is] not. This [is] the portion of them that spoil us, and the lot of them that rob us."* Isaiah 17:13-14

The multi-national invasion of Israel is frustrated in the attempt to rob and take spoil from the country. These nations use the Israeli invasion of Syria as an excuse to attack the land of Israel, but in reality they have another agenda.

In Ezekiel 38 we read about the invasion of the modern nation of Israel. We know it is the modern nation from 38:8. The nation of Israel has allies; two of which are in the Middle East, Egypt and Saudi Arabia. All of the allies question the motives of the invaders and accuse them in 38:13 of coming *"to take a spoil"* just as we read in Isaiah 17. The other allies are described as the *"merchants of Tarshish[8] and the young lions thereof"*.

We cannot identify the location of Tarshish with any certainty. If the Tarshish in view was located on the British Isles, then the merchants of Tarshish and the young lions thereof would refer to England, Scotland, Wales, Ireland, Canada, America, New Zeeland and Australia. These nations are currently allies of the land of Israel. The year that the United Nations, under the influence of the Islamic conspiracy, endorses a full-scale attack on Israel, her allies will boycott the Olympics.

The nation of Magog[9] is depicted as coming against Israel equipped with both offensive and defensive weapons (Ezekiel 38:4). Magog is identified as referring to the former USSR.

In 38:14-16, the invading nation attacks from the north. The Commonwealth of Independent States including the Islamic countries of Estonia, Latvia, Lithuania, Kazakhstan, Kyrgyzstan and Afghanistan, would be included in this geographical derivation.

In Ezekiel 38:5 we see Persia, Ethiopia and Libya equipped with defensive weapons. Persia would constitute the Islamic nations to the East of Israel, while Ethiopia would refer to the Islamic countries of North Africa, to the South of Israel. In verse 6 Gomer and Togarmah are mentioned, which refers to Turkey and the European countries. All the Islamic nations that surround modern Israel are pictured in the invasion, with the exception of Syria. The possibility is that Syria is not mentioned because it will have been neutralized by Israel and would be the published reason behind the multi-national assault on the Jewish State.

In Ezekiel 39:3 we see that the invading armies are destroyed by the intervention of God. The destruction is of such a magnitude that they bury the dead for 7 months (39:12) and burn the war weapons for fuel for seven years (39:9). Many feel that these events will take place during the tribulation but it seems unlikely to me that Israel will still be using the weapons for fuel in the kingdom age. It also seems contradictory to watch Israel bury the war dead for seven months while they are also fleeing from the persecution of the end time world ruler. Perhaps the Ezekiel 38 war will take place before the great tribulation. This war could easily be a catalyst for the events of the great tribulation. If this war does involve the Islamic countries, the defeat and destruction of Islam will pave the way for the rebuilding of the Temple, mentioned in Matthew 24:15.

After the horrific slaughter in this war, the world just might be persuaded to move towards some sort of universal disarmament. The subjects of the world might be ready to sacrifice freedom for safety and universally agree to capitulate to a one-world ruler; one who will guarantee universal peace.

He will divide the globe into ten nations for the purpose of government. These ethnic derivations will involve the relocation of almost everyone and the Jewish people will be awarded the Holy Land primarily due to the fact they were the victors. The ruler will establish a universal government - a one world, economic cashless system, a single religion and a single language. Once he is ensconced in power and the Jewish people have all been settled in the land, he will begin his campaign to destroy the Jewish people of the world.

In order to be certain that every Jew has been killed, Satan must be in complete control of the world and the world systems. He will use his power and resources to attempt to annihilate the Jewish people to prevent the confession, which will pave the way for the Messiah's return. His attempt will actually drive the Jewish people to seek the Lord early and to gaze upon the one whom they have pierced.

> *I will go [and] return to my place, till they acknowledge their offence, and seek my face: in their affliction they will seek me early."* Hosea 5:15

> *"And I will pour upon the house of David, and upon the inhabitants of Jerusalem, the spirit of grace and of supplications: and they shall look upon me whom they have pierced, and they shall mourn for him, as one mourneth for [his] only [son], and shall be in bitterness for him, as one that is in bitterness for [his] firstborn."* Zechariah 12:10

In seeking the Lord, the Jewish people will look back at the crucifixion and acknowledge their national rejection of the Messiah. Zechariah 12:9 tells us that the Lord will destroy all the nations that come against Jerusalem. Verse 11 says that there will be great mourning in the valley of Megiddon, like the mourning that occurred when Josiah the king of Judah was slain as recorded in 2 Chronicles 35:22-25. In Revelation 16 we see the armies of the world gathered together at Armageddon.[10] Following this gathering at Armageddon, we read about an earthquake of unprecedented proportions, that divides the city of Jerusalem into three parts.

Okay, let us see if we can put the facts from Revelation 16 together with Zechariah in sequential order. The armies of the world are gathered against the Jews at Armageddon. Those armies sweep down to the south and in Zechariah 13:8 we read how two parts, which I assume is two thirds of the Jewish people, will be cut off and die. The one third that is left will be refined through fire in the city of Jerusalem.

> *"For I will gather all nations against Jerusalem to battle; and the city shall be taken, and the houses rifled, and the women ravished;*

> *and half of the city shall go forth into captivity[11], and the residue of the people shall not be cut off from the city."* Zechariah 14:2

The nations that have gathered against Israel in Megiddo in the north sweep south into Jerusalem. In the campaign, two thirds of the Jewish people are wiped out in what will be the worst horror of the nation's incredibly horrible history. Then, at Jerusalem, all the nations gather again to do battle and they take the city. The language of Zechariah 14:2 is a bit complicated. The expression half the city is taken away is not referring to captivity, but is probably referring to the events of the succeeding verses.

> *"Then shall the LORD go forth, and fight against those nations, as when he fought in the day of battle. And his feet shall stand in that day upon the mount of Olives, which [is] before Jerusalem on the east, and the mount of Olives shall cleave in the midst thereof toward the east and toward the west, [and there shall be] a very great valley; and half of the mountain shall remove toward the north, and half of it toward the south."* Zechariah 14:3-4

The Lord returns to the Mount of Olives according to the promise of the two angels in Acts 1:9-12. The occasion of the Lord's return accompanies the great earthquake of Revelation 16:18. The mountain is divided in half, just like the promise of Matthew 17:20. The city is divided into three parts by the earthquake. One part is half the city and the other two parts make up the other half. The division of the mountain and the city provides a way of escape for the Jewish people who have remained alive during the onslaught. They escape to the valley of the mountains as they did at the time of Uzziah's earthquake. The valley of the mountains extends to Azal according to Zechariah 14:5.

The Provided Place

In Revelation 12, we read of the historic war that the adversary has been waging against the Jewish people for centuries. We read about his attempt to destroy the Messiah at the first advent in verse 4 and then we see the attempt to destroy the nation to prohibit the Second Coming. A portion of the nation of Israel flees to the wilderness following the instructions of Matthew 24:16-20.

In Revelation 12:6 and 14 we read about how God provides for those Jewish people and protects them for three and a half years, while they wait for those Jewish people who will be delivered from the siege on Jerusalem by means of the great earthquake. Both verses refer to "her place" which is in the wilderness according to Revelation 12 and is called the "valley of the mountains" in Zechariah 14.

We see Jesus returning to the Mount of Olives with the purpose of fighting against the nations (Zechariah 14:3). In 14:2 all the nations were gathered against Jerusalem. We have not been told where the valley of the mountains is. We know it is in the wilderness and that all the armies of all the nations are going to chase after the surviving Jewish people. Where the Jewish people go, the armies of the Antichrist will follow. We also know that wherever the armies are, that is where the Lord will be since He returns to fight those nations.

In Isaiah 34 we see the indignation of the Lord is upon all nations and His fury is upon all their armies. The utter destruction of these armies proves that this must be the place. The place is Bozra in Edom, or as we would refer to the territory on today's maps, Petra in South Jordan. An earlier civilization had carved apartments into the rocks, which left a safe haven for the hiding Jewish people. The mountain caves that are there meet the criteria of being a valley of the mountain and a wilderness. All the armies of the world are utterly destroyed at this location. We have always been taught that the destruction of the world's armies takes place at the battle of Armageddon. Isaiah 34:2 makes it clear that the armies are destroyed and 34:6 clarifies the place of the destruction as being Bozrah.

All the armies were gathered at Armageddon and there is to be a horrific destruction at that location. However, the destruction appears to be the annihilation of two thirds of the Jewish people in the Armageddon campaign. The armies will follow the Jewish retreat to Jerusalem and put a siege on the city. The return of the Lord will allow the Jewish people to escape by means of an earth splitting quake. Israel will flee to the place that Lord has provided for her and the armies of the world will pursue her to her place.

There in Bozrah, all the armies, of all the nations, will finally be destroyed. So, in reality there is no battle of Armageddon. Well at least it does not appear to take place at Armageddon. In Isaiah 63:1-4 we see the Lord returning from Bozrah after the destruction of the armies of the world. There was no battle there either since a battle involves a conflict. There was no conflict and the outcome was never in doubt. The Lord single handedly destroys all the armed forces of the entire world at the place He provided for His people.

The Pre-Millennial Pronouncement

"If they shall confess their iniquity, and the iniquity of their fathers, with their trespass which they trespassed against me, and that also they have walked contrary unto me; And [that] I also have walked contrary unto them, and have brought them into the land of their enemies; if then their uncircumcised hearts be humbled, and they then accept of the punishment of their iniquity: Then will I remember my covenant with Jacob, and also my covenant with Isaac, and also my covenant with Abraham will I remember; and I will remember the land." Leviticus 26:40-42

In the first 12 verses of Leviticus 26 we read about the blessings that the Lord will bestow upon His ancient people if they keep the commandments. The blessings included are in four realms. First, the Jewish people will be blessed spiritually. God will respect them, set His tabernacle among them and walk among them. Next, in the personal realm, the Jewish people will be fruitful and will enjoy peace. Thirdly, in the area of agriculture, the Jewish people can expect ample rainfall, fruitful land, plentiful and productive fruit-bearing trees, great crops of grain and abundant vineyards.

If a nation in the middle of other nations is enjoying all of these physical blessings and the surrounding nations are not, there needs to be one final blessing and that would be in the area of the military. And so fourthly, the Lord promises that the Jewish people will chase their enemies and that their land will not be destroyed. These blessings belong to the chosen people if they continue to behave in obedience towards the Lord.

The Jewish people failed to keep God's commandments. In Leviticus 26:13-39 we read about the consequences of disobedience. As we discussed earlier, the Lord allows the Jewish people to go through five phases or cycles of discipline. Each cycle is more severe than the previous one and at the conclusion of each cycle there is a challenge from the Lord to repent.

The fifth cycle of discipline is a bit complex, but it clearly includes the Babylonian captivity, and it also goes beyond that to describe the ultimate dispersion which lasts from 70 A.D. until the establishment of the modern nation of Israel.

In Leviticus 26:40, the ultimate opportunity to repent is extended to the Jewish people. In verse 41, the Lord requires that the confession include an acknowledgement of the fact that the Lord walked contrary unto them because of their iniquity, even the iniquity of their fathers. The Chumash completely mistranslates 26:41.

"I, too, will behave towards them with casualness and I will bring them into the land of their enemies-perhaps then their unfeeling heart will be humbled and then they will gain appeasement for their sin."[12]
In the ensuing discussion the Chumash says, *"the commentators wonder why the repentance of verse 40 should be greeted with this outpouring of wrath"*.

In actuality, the confession of Leviticus 26:40 is not met with wrath. The wrath described there is part of the confession and the

Jewish people must recognize that the horrific things that have befallen them through the years were the consequences of the transgression of their fathers. They must acknowledge that the wrath of God was deserved. This fact is difficult to recognize and even more difficult to discuss. It can only be spiritually discerned.

Recently, we were blessed to see a beautiful 74-year young Jewish lady come to trust in her Messiah and just a week later she was attending a Passover Seder. At the meal a man asked why Jewish people suffer so much? Our new believer, without any training, without ever having attended church, responded with, "Don't you get it? Don't you understand it? They rejected their Messiah." The Holy Spirit revealed it to her, a simple fact that is so tremendously difficult to accept.

When the idea is proffered that the unbelief of Jewish people could actually be responsible for the holocaust, the response is to accuse anyone who would hold to such an idea as being the worst kind of anti-Semite. Yet the Chumash actually refers to that conclusion as a possible way of understanding the difficult language of Leviticus 26:40 and 41.

The Chumash offers two possible explanations. The first is that the confession of the Jewish people was insincere. As evidence in support of that view, the Chumash mentions the following: *"When King Cyrus of Persia gave permission to the Jews to return to the Land, only 42,360 did so (Ezra 2:64) a pitifully small percentage of the nation and all through the years of the Second Temple, the majority of Jews lived elsewhere."*[13]

The second possibility mentioned in the Chumash is the one that is Spiritually revealed, *"both verses are part of the confession and lists the truths that Israel must acknowledge before their repentance can be considered genuine."*[14] Before the Lord will restore the covenant that He made with the patriarchs, the Jewish people must confess the transgression of their fathers and acknowledge all the consequences and ramifications of that transgression as well.

> *"Only acknowledge thine iniquity, that thou hast transgressed against the Lord thy God and hast scattered thy ways to the strangers under every green tree and you have not obeyed my voice saith the Lord."* Jeremiah 3:13

Jeremiah 3:14-19 describes the restoration of the nation of Israel. The language shows us that this reformation is not referring to the incidents of 1948 and 1967, but of the yet future and complete restoration of the kingdom. God refers to Himself as the husband of Israel in verse 14. In verse 15, He promises to give shepherds or pastors who are men after God's own heart. In 3:17, Jerusalem will be established as the throne of the Lord and all nations shall be gathered to it. In verse 18, Israel and Judah are united and receive the inheritance of the fathers. In 3:19 they are promised a goodly heritage of the hosts of the nations and they shall call Him father and never turn away from Him again. Those events will only occur in the Kingdom and this Kingdom in Jeremiah will be established only if the nation acknowledges its iniquity.

The same word for iniquity appears both in Jeremiah 3:13 and in Leviticus 26:40. In both passages the word is singular. In order for the kingdom to be established the Jewish people must confess a singular iniquity of their fathers. The question is, "What is the iniquity?"

The fathers lost the Bible for years and failed to keep the Sabbath. Also, they made alliances with immoral nations, built groves unto Baal and caused their children to pass through the fire; further, they failed to take advantage of the opportunity to repent and ended up in Babylonian captivity. When the Lord allowed them to return, only a small percentage chose to do so. There must have been millions of transgressions perpetrated by millions of people over a period of several hundred years. What single sin needs to be confessed?

Are We There Yet?

I often ask religious Jewish people to consider the following facts. The Jewish people entered the Promised Land under Joshua around 1400 years before Jesus. The Babylonian captivity began in 586 B.C. The time of the Judges and the Kings together totals about 800 years. The Jewish people were in the land for a total of approximately 800 years. After 800 years of disobeying the Lord, the nation faced 70 years of punishment.

They returned from the Babylonian captivity in 516 B.C. In 70 A.D. the nation of Israel was dispersed and the punishment lasted 1,878 years. When 800 years of disobedience results in 70 years of punishment, what could they have done in the ensuing 585[15] years that would result in 1,878 years of punishment? [16] Or to repeat the earlier question, "What single sin do they need to confess?" A single iniquity, according to Leviticus 26 resulted in the Diaspora and ultimately the Holocaust. In Hosea 5 we read about this concept again. Again the Jewish people need to recognize a single offense and as a result the Kingdom would be established.

> *"I will go and return to my place, till they acknowledge their offence, and seek my face: in their affliction they will seek me early."* Hosea 5:15

The Lord is speaking and He says that he is going to return to heaven. This verse proves Jesus is the LORD. In order for God to return to heaven, He must have left heaven. Jesus is the one who left heaven and came to earth. He will stay in heaven until the Jewish people acknowledge their offence. Again a single sin needs to be acknowledged before the Lord will return. This verse not only establishes Jesus as the LORD, but it also reaffirms the need for and the reality of Israel's premillennial pronouncement.

That sin which was not forgiven, in the next age (the age to come, which is the church age) will be forgiven. That sin, once confessed and acknowledged after the church is removed and the tribulation has begun, will be forgiven.

"Then answered all the people and said, His blood (be) on us, and on our children." Matthew 27:25

"it shall not be forgiven him, neither in this world, neither in the (world) to come." Matthew 12:32

Remember, the tribulation is the continuation of the 70 weeks of Daniel. One of the six things that Daniel predicted for those seventy weeks was to make an end of the transgression. The singular transgression has come to its end.

"Comfort ye, comfort ye my people, saith your God. Speak ye comfortably to Jerusalem and cry unto her, that her warfare is accomplished, that her iniquity is pardoned:" Isaiah 40:1-2

Her single iniquity is pardoned. We know that part of the pronouncement of Israel's confession is to include the words of Psalm 118:26, *"Blessed (be) he that cometh in the name of the Lord:"* We know from Zechariah 12:10 that the confession will involve a national heart of remorse concerning the Son of God. I think we can also find the exact words of the confession recorded for us in the Scriptures.

The 53rd chapter of Isaiah was written some 700 years before the cross. If he was looking forward to the cross, you would expect his writing to appear in the future tense, but Isaiah writes the passage about the cross work of the Messiah in the past tense. He is not predicting the cross: he is recording Israel's national confession of the cross. When Israel is surrounded by the armies of the world at Bozrah in Petra, they will gaze back upon the one whom they have pierced and will make their premillennial pronouncement.

Israel confesses, *"He was despised... and we esteemed him not. Surely he hath borne our griefs, and carried our sorrows: yet we did esteem him stricken, smitten of God, and afflicted. But he (was) wounded for our transgressions, (he was) bruised for our iniquities: the chastisement of our peace (was) upon him; and with his stripes we are healed. All we like sheep have gone astray; we have turned every one to his own way; and the Lord hath laid on him the iniquity of us all"* Isaiah 53:3-6. In verse eight we continue to read *"he was cut off out of the land of the living: for the transgression of my people was he stricken."*

Upon the confession of the nation of Israel the Lord defeats the armies of the world surrounding the Jewish people at Bozrah (Isaiah 34:1-6), and returns (Isaiah 63:1) to establish the year of the redeemed (Isaiah 63:4). Then the long awaited kingdom will begin.

CHAPTER FIVE

Jacob's Trouble

"And there shall be a time of trouble, such as never was since there was a nation." Daniel 12:1

This unprecedented time of trouble is referred to as *"the time of Jacob's trouble"* in Jeremiah 30:7. It belongs to Israel; they earned it. It is during the tribulation that the end time ruler is going to attempt to annihilate all the Jewish people (Matthew 24:9).

Once the restraining power of the Church has been removed (2 Thessalonians 2:6-7) at the occasion of the rapture (2 Thessalonians 2:1),[1] the end time ruler can pursue his ambitions of the total annihilation of Israel. He of course, will fail and in his attempt to destroy the Jewish people and will actually precipitate his own destruction.

The abbreviated seven-year period (Matthew 24:22), the seventieth week of Daniel's prophecy, is mostly concerned with the nation of Israel. However, in order for the end time ruler to be certain of total Jewish elimination, he must have worldwide domination. So, although the Great Tribulation is for the most part limited in scope to the land of Israel and the surrounding nations, it will certainly have global repercussions.[2]

When we studied the signs, we had the benefit of hindsight and could refer to almanacs and encyclopedias. When we studied famines and earthquakes, we could look at the writings of the rabbis to assist us. As we approach the study of the tribulation, however, we do not have the advantage of looking back. It is difficult to define the events with certainty, so we will be forced to read from the scriptures themselves. A rather novel concept, but bear with me.

The Gentile Beast

The end time ruler has at least fifteen different names in the Scriptures. Isaiah calls him *"the Assyrian"* in 10:24; 30:31; 31:8, *"the wicked"* in 11:4, *"the king of Babylon"* in 14:4, *"the spoiler"* and *"the extortioner"* in 16:4.

Daniel refers to him as, *"the little horn"* in 7:8 and 8:9; *"the beast"* in 7:11, *"the king of fierce countenance"* in 8:23, *"the king of the north"* in 11:6 and *"the king"* in 11:36.

Jesus called him *"the abomination of desolation"* in Matthew 24:15 and Paul referred to him as *"the man of sin; the son of perdition"* and *"that Wicked"* in 2 Thessalonians 2:3-8. In 1 John 2:18 he is called *"the antichrist"*. The term *"antichrist"* is only used four times in the Scriptures, all in the epistles of John (1 John 2:18, 22; 4:3; 2 John 1:7), yet that term seems to be the most popular of all.

Of the 15 different titles that he has, I dislike the term antichrist the most. First and foremost, because I always feel like it should be hyphenated; it never looks right when I spell it. Secondly, as a Jewish believer it took me years to embrace the term Christ. I had to overcome a lot of baggage. I have taught myself to love the term Christ and now I dislike seeing Christ in the name of the enemy in any format.

Of the fifteen different titles that the Scriptures give him, Isaiah gives him five. The focus of Isaiah seems to be on the ultimate defeat of the enemy of God's people. The Assyrian is destroyed in 10:25-27, *"beaten down...with a rod"* in 30:31, and falls from a sword in 31:8. The Lord slays the one who is called, the wicked, with *"the breath of his lips"* in 11:4.

The ultimate ruin and total humiliation of the king of Babylon is described in 14:4-11. The spoiler will cease and the extortioner is at an end in 16:4. The rod that beats him, the sword that causes him to fall and the breath of the Lord that slays him have reference to the Word of the Lord.

Although Isaiah makes certain of the ultimate end of the enemy, he does not ignore the horror of his reign. In 10:24 the Lord tells the people who are returned and dwelling in Zion not to be afraid of the Assyrian.

> *"O my people that dwellest in Zion, be not afraid of the Assyrian: he shall smite thee with a rod and shall lift up his staff against thee after the manner of Egypt."* Isaiah 10:24

The Jewish people are encouraged by the ultimate destruction of the Assyrian not to fear his temporary reign. However, even in the encouragement we read how he will smite the Jewish people with his rod. There is also a reference to his staff after the manner of Egypt which sounds like some kind of enslavement. That makes sense. The Assyrian has an agenda to kill all the Jews. The rest of the world has to be brought into line with his program. Enslaving the Jewish people dehumanizes them making it easier to persecute them and finally rid the world of them.

As he takes power and begins his persecution, the Jewish people will start to flee to the wilderness. This will take them through Moab and so, in Isaiah 16:4, the Lord asks Moab to cover the fleeing Jews from the face of the spoiler.

The language of 16:4 fascinates me. The Lord mentions to Moab that the extortioner has come to an end. Moab may have been inclined to be merciful to the persecuted Jews, but in fear of reprisal from the spoiler/extortioner they were reluctant to act on righteous inclinations.

So the Lord tells them they can continue to do the right things without future fears. I am fascinated because it makes me think of the Holocaust. I am wondering how many believers, knowing the right thing, knowing the eternal God, chose to fear a temporary spoiler, and lifted not a finger to protect, nor a whisper to protest the slaughter of the chosen people of that eternal God.

In Isaiah 14:4 the end time ruler is called *"the king of Babylon"*. Here, along with the focus on his destruction, the prophet speaks mostly to the contrast of the one time mighty ruler being brought to nothing. I am captivated by 14:6 where we read of the irony that the one time popular world ruler is now persecuted and apparently there is not a single person willing to hinder the process.

I find this verse interesting on two counts. The use of the word hinder reminds me of 2 Thessalonians 2 where we see the Church in the role of the restrainer, who will hinder the activity of the wicked until the rapture. Now, in Isaiah 14:6 we see the end of the wicked and there is no one found to hinder his persecution.

The second thing that I find ironic about this verse is the mention of loneliness. The most powerful and popular man in the world dies alone without support and without an ally. He was once worshipped as God, and now he is tormented, alone. It reminds me of Isaiah 63:5.

Upon his return from the destruction of all the armies of the world that had gathered together to destroy the Jewish people, Jesus seems to marvel that He had to fight the battle alone. He wondered at the fact that there was no one to uphold his arm. I find it intriguing that the two greatest combatants of all time (if Jesus can be truly seen as a combatant) face each other alone; not a single soul will support either. Because of fear, every man has abandoned his beliefs and principles and arrives at a position of neutrality and compromise.

Like Isaiah, the prophet Daniel also has given the end time ruler five different titles as we mentioned above. He is called the *"little horn"* in 7:8 and 8:9. Also in 8:23 he is called *"king of fierce countenance"*. He is *"the prince that shall come"* in 9:26-27, *"the king of the north"* in 11:5-40 and *"the beast"* in 7:11.

The first reference to him in the book of Daniel is in chapter 7. Here the prophet records his vision of the four beasts coming out of the sea. According to the angelic interpretation in 7:17, these four beasts represent Gentile national rulers. The fourth beast is a picture of the old Roman Empire, the fourth of the four successive kingdoms to rule over the ancient world.

> *"After this I saw in the night visions, and behold a fourth beast, dreadful and terrible, and strong exceedingly; and it had great iron teeth: it devoured and brake in pieces, and stamped the residue with the feet of it: and it [was] diverse from all the beasts that [were] before it; and it had ten horns."* Daniel 7:7

The other beasts are described as a lion, a leopard and a bear; this beast is not described. The indescribable fourth beast has nothing on earth to which it might be compared. It is said to be dreadful, terrible and of great strength. The iron teeth symbolize the same iron of 2:40-43. It devours all the previous beasts and stamps upon them with its feet. This means that the fourth beast conquers all the territories of the previous empires.

This beast is different from all the others and the ancient Roman Empire differed in that it was a republican form of government. It differed in power greatness, in extent of dominion and in length of duration. The ten horns symbolize ten final day rulers.[3]

> *I considered the horns, and, behold, there came up among them another little horn, before whom there were three of the first horns plucked up by the roots: and, behold, in this horn [were] eyes like the eyes of man, and a mouth speaking great things.*[4] Daniel 7:8

After the other ten rulers are established, another king arises among them. This king will pluck up three of the existing kings, symbolic of a military overthrow. The remaining submit to him without further warfare.

Are We There Yet?

I have no idea why the Scriptures give so much detail regarding the number of kings involved in the events that lead to the worldwide dominion of the little horn. Daniel 7 clearly explains the symbolism. When these events begin to unfold, the people who are alive at that time should have little trouble identifying the characters and players. Perhaps precise identification is necessary, because the character of the little horn will seem to be so dynamic that in the beginning it will be difficult for the Bible reader to believe that the bad guy is all that bad.

> *" And he shall speak [great] words against the most High, and shall wear out[5] the saints of the most High, and think to change times and laws: and they shall be given into his hand until a time and times and the dividing of time."* Daniel 7:25

The power of persuasive speech always amazes me. A good speaker can sway a crowd emotionally without saying anything substantial. As a mediocre speaker, it makes me jealous to listen to some of these guys and to observe the response from the audience. A loud and timely shout will always elicit a hearty amen from the congregation, even when the words themselves are relatively meaningless. The great words here are blasphemous words spoken against the most High.

I was depositing a check from Friends of Israel recently and the teller asked about the organization. It is rare that we ever have time to discuss things at the bank because usually, the line of waiting people forces us to run in and get out without inconveniencing the crowd behind us. This moment was unusual as the bank was, besides the employees and myself, completely empty.

When the teller asked about the organization, I assumed she was a believer and I confidently shared my testimony with her. Funny how that works. We are quicker to share when we expect a positive response. Well, I was in for a shock. Not only was the teller not saved; she was adamantly in opposition to the things of the Lord.

I was taken aback, for two reasons. The first was that tellers are usually so concerned about public relations that they go overboard to say and do things to please the customer. As a people group, I would list bank tellers as one of the least likely to offend.

The second thing that caught me off guard was that, in addition to her confrontational demeanor in attacking my faith, she was extremely bold in her attack on the character of Jesus. I can remember a time when everyone, including people without faith, had respect unto the Lord. She called Jesus a fraud and a coward and was quick to render evidence to substantiate her position.

The atmosphere in this country has changed. And from what I am told, things are better here than in most other countries. The day is coming when a worldwide ruler will gain respect and popularity with blasphemy.

In addition to the reference to blasphemy, Daniel 7:25 says that the beast *"will wear out the saints"*. The beast will have the audacity to speak against God and to persecute the people of God. The saints of the tribulation are the Jewish people. And the unconditional promise to Abraham is still in effect. The beast will curse the seed of Abraham for a season, but in the end God will curse the beast.

Along with the things the beast will do, 7:25 also mentions that he will *"think to change the times and the laws"*.[6] As powerful as the beast is, he is not omnipotent and there apparently are things that he purposes to do, but is incapable of accomplishing.

> *"And in the latter time of their kingdom, when the transgressors are come to the full, a king of fierce countenance and understanding dark sentences, shall stand up."* Daniel 8:23

Daniel describes the end time ruler as *"dreadful and terrible"* in 7:7. In 7:8, Daniel mentions the eyes of a man in the beast, which is a reference to the intelligence of the beast. The desire *"to change the times and the laws"* is a reference to something that is probably evil.

The understanding of *"dark sentences"* is definitely a reference to something evil. At first glance that sounds like a reference to spells or incantations, but I cannot find anything in Judaica or in the literature of Mesopotamia to collaborate it.

We know that the end time ruler is a great talker and we know that men love darkness rather than light. A great talker will know how to wield the dark sentences to manipulate the audience. The end time ruler will be a skilled, evil raconteur who will wield his persuasive powers to gain massive popularity.

In Revelation 13:3, *"the whole world wondered after the beast and worshiped the beast"*. Somewhere in the history of the beast there will be a miraculous recovery. He will either be near death or perhaps even resurrected from death (Revelation 13:3,12). But I do not think the universal admiration is going to be a response to the miracles or accomplishments. Those things can attract attention, but that kind of universal approbation and veneration can only be stimulated by meaningless, unsubstantiated dark and deceptive rhetoric.

The end time ruler is called *"the prince that shall come"* in Daniel 9:26. The people of that prince will be the same people who destroy the city of Jerusalem and the sanctuary of the Holy Temple.

In the year 70 A.D. the Roman people entered into Jerusalem to end a Jewish rebellion. At that time they destroyed both the city and the sanctuary. The end time ruler is to be of the same people who destroyed Jerusalem. Hence, the end time ruler has to be in some way defined as Roman. He might come from Rome; he might be Italian; he might be European; he might be Roman Catholic, but one thing is certain; he is not Jewish.

In Daniel 11:6 we are introduced to the king of the North. The entire chapter of Daniel 11 is prophetic. Some of the prophecy is so specific that people believe it was written after the event, as history. Most of the passage deals with events that occur within four hundred years after the writing of Daniel.

Each of those historic kings mentioned are typical of the end time ruler and the last several verses of the chapter seem to deal with him specifically and solely.

In Daniel 11:13-19 the king of the north is Antiochus the Great. He ascended the throne of Syria in 223 BC and was succeeded by his son Seleucus Philopater in 187 BC (Daniel 11:20). Antiochus the IV, who is surnamed Epiphanies,[7][8] succeeded his brother Seleucus in 175. Daniel prophetically predicts the career and character of Antiochus Epiphanies in 11:21-32.

> *"And in his estate shall stand up a vile person, to whom they shall not give the honour of the kingdom: but he shall come in peaceably, and obtain the kingdom by flatteries."* Daniel 11:21

Antiochus was on his way from Rome when his brother Seleucus died. Heliodorus, who poisoned Seleucus, had already declared himself to be king and, fortunately for Antiochus, so had several others. None of the self appointed kings had clear title so there was no single person or party to attack. Antiochus therefore, returned to the city peaceably. He used flattery to win the support of his other brothers and the support of Eumenes the king of Pergamos.

He flattered the Romans by sending them ambassadors with tribute money that was in arrears. He won the favor of the Syrian people by hanging out with the common people, drinking and singing songs of debauchery in taverns. He is a new kind of leader and typifies the end time rulers like Bill Clinton and the antichrist.

Many character descriptions of these historical kings can be used to describe the antichrist as well. *"His heart shall be lifted up"* 11:12 and he acts *"according to his own will"* in verse 16. Antiochus is described as a *"vile person"* of flatteries in verse 21, one who used deceit in verse 23 and extensive bribery in verse 24.

In addition to similarities in character, Antiochus typifies the end time ruler in his behavior. Both defile the altar in the holiest of places beyond the veil (Daniel 11:21, Matthew 24:15). Both express total defiance toward the Lord God and His ancient people and both conduct unsuccessful military campaigns against the Jewish people.

> *"And (some) of them of understanding shall fall to try them, and to purge, and to make (them) white, (even) to the time of the end: because (it is) yet for a time appointed."* Daniel 11:35

I just love the KJV.[9] I do not think it is based on a superior text and I do not think it is the most accurate of the translations. The reason I love it is for verses like Daniel 11:35. See, a verse like that just has to be explained. It is so very obscure that it requires a teacher and it keeps me employed. It should read something like this: *"and some of those who have understanding will fall into persecution, through this persecution they will be refined and cleansed and made pure until the time of the end, for the appointed time is still to come"*.

The verse begins speaking of the Maccabees, but concludes with a reference to the appointed end time. In both the rebellion against Antiochus and in the tribulation, the Jewish people are purged through suffering. However, the very purpose of the tribulation is the cleansing of the nation for the kingdom. Mention of the appointed time of the end seems to direct our focus away from Antiochus and the near history to the end time ruler of the tribulation.

The remainder of Daniel 11 seems to speak to the end time ruler exclusively. In 11:36 we read that he will do according to his own will. We know that the end time ruler is a willful king; however we also know that he is not omnipotent and there are things that he wishes to do but is unable to accomplish. In 11:37 he exalts and magnifies himself above every god (2 Thessalonians 2:4).

> *"Neither shall he regard the God of his fathers, nor the desire of women, nor regard any god: for he shall magnify himself above all."* Daniel 11:37

The expression *"God of his fathers"* seems to indicate the God of Abraham, Isaac and Jacob. And it points to a Jewish end time ruler. However, we learned from Daniel 9:26 that the prince that shall come has to be a Roman. If he is indeed a Roman Catholic, the expression *"God of his fathers"* would still be referring to rejection of the God of Abraham, since the Roman church embraces the same God. The phrase *"desire of women"* is not a reference to celibacy nor is it referring to male homosexuality, rather it is probably referring to the desire that women have to bear the Messiah.

So the end time ruler will reject the God of Abraham, will have no respect for the Messiah and will exalt himself above all false gods as well (2 Thessalonians 2:4). However, he does have respect for the *"god of forces"* (Daniel 11:38) and he brings precious metals in tribute to honor to him. The god of forces is Satan. He is the prince of the power of the air (Ephesians 2:2) and he is the god of this world (2 Corinthians 4:4). Satan is described as a strange god in 11:39

In Deuteronomy 13, the Jewish people are warned about *"a dreamer of dreams"* who works wonders and attempts to cause them to follow after other gods The Jewish people are admonished to put this wonder working false prophet to death (Deuteronomy 13:5). Some people believe that this passage is referring to Jesus and that Jesus was a test to see if the Jewish people would remain loyal. Jesus did work wonders, but He worked these wonders in the name of the Father and directed the Jewish people to Him (John 12:48-50).

"I am come in my father's name, and ye receive me not: if another shall come in his own name, him ye will receive" John 5:43

The beast spoken of in Daniel 7 reappears in Revelation 13. In John's vision he arises out of the sea. The Mediterranean is the access to the nations and because of that, references to the sea often typify the Gentiles. This beast has seven heads, which represent the seven remaining nations that capitulate to the beast after three of the original ten nations were defeated in warfare.

The ten horns of the beast are the ten individual rulers of the ten nations and the crowns are the indications of the authority that would belong to the heads of state. The dragon gives this Gentile beast his power. The dragon is identified clearly as Satan (Revelation 12:9).

The whole Gentile world worships the beast and Satan who gives the beast his power (Revelation 13:4). But that is not enough for him. His desire is to receive the adoration of the chosen people of God, but the Jewish people will never acquiesce to a Gentile ruler. They must first be enticed by one of their own.

He eventually will enter the Holy of Holies and set himself up as god (2 Thessalonians 2:4). Then, even though they except him and worship him, he still cannot trust them to stay loyal. I think he will attempt changes in the Jewish liturgical calendar and will fail (Daniel 7:25). His insecurity will throw him into a rage. Then he will begin the Armageddon campaign in earnest (Revelation 16:16).

But first the dreamer of dreams, the worker of wonders must appear on the scene and lead the Jewish people to a god that their fathers did not know. And so in fulfillment of Deuteronomy 13, we see the advent of the second beast who deceives the Jewish People. One beast is enough for the Goyim, they drink, but we Jews are sober so we need two beasts.

The Jewish Beast

"And I beheld another beast coming up out of the earth; and he had two horns like a lamb, and he spake as a dragon. And he exerciseth all the power of the first beast before him, and causeth the earth and them which dwell therein to worship the first beast, whose deadly wound was healed" Revelation 13:11-12

The second beast is seen coming out of the earth. This is a picture of the land of Israel.[10] The two horns represent the leaders of a united Israel and Judah. He looks Jewish, but he talks just like the devil. He wields the same power of the first beast. Both beasts are men. Neither beast is Satan, although both beasts are empowered by Satan.

The restrainer of evil has been removed at the rapture (2 Thessalonians 2:6-7). Without the Holy Spirit, the beast will easily seduce the Gentile world. Whatever opposition there might be, it will fall quickly to the delusion sent from God (2 Thessalonians 2:11).

The Gentiles seek after the wisdom of the flattering words of the glib beast. While the Jews require a sign (1 Corinthians 1:22). The second beast will provide the wondrous signs to complete the dog and pony show. He causes the entire population of Israel to worship the first beast.[11]

The Jewish people are not quickly going to embrace a Gentile leader. The Jewish people are looking for the Jewish Messiah. The second beast will assume that role. He will be Jewish and he more than the first beast will be the false messiah, the one who should be called antichrist.

This Jewish false messiah will be the wonder worker of Deuteronomy 13. He will make an image of the first beast, cause that image to live and give it the ability to speak (Revelation 13:14-15). He will bring fire down from heaven just like Elijah did at the great confrontation with the prophets of Baal in 1 Kings 18 (Revelation 13:13). Then he will cause the Jewish people to worship the first beast (Revelation 13:12), and all the Jewish people who refuse to worship the image of the beast that he made will be put to death (Revelation 13:15).

A similar scenario occurred at the time of the Maccabees. *"Antiochus, who was mad, bad and dangerous, sold the high-priesthood to the highest bidder, one Menelaus, who was quite unentitled to it and when in 168 BC, his nominee was ejected, Aniochus sent his officer to sack Jerusalem and kill its inhabitants.*

Soon afterwards, Antiochus instituted a religious persecution of unprecedented bitterness. Sabbath keeping and the practice of circumcision were forbidden under pain of death: pagan sacrifices and prostitution were established in the Temple; and law-loving Jews were subjected to every degradation and brutality."[12]

I quoted the previous few lines directly from the encyclopedia to show that the extent of the deprivation and the dreadful conditions were not exaggerated by my Jewish subjectivity. Antiochus defiled the Temple by slaughtering a pig in it. Prior to that he set up what was supposed to be an image of Zeus on the altar, but in reality it was an image of Antiochus. In a city called Modein, a Jewish man volunteered to participate in the political sacrifice. In a rage an old man named Mattathias slew the Jewish infidel and the Syrian official on guard and formally started the Jewish rebellion.

In the end time events another image is going to be set up in the Temple and again the Jewish people who refuse to buckle under will face degradation and death. At the time of Antiochus, the Jewish leaders fought the Syrians and slew the Jewish people who capitulated. At the end time, the Jewish leader will slay fellow Jews who fail to submit. This Jewish beast will be, for Israel, the forerunner, as the first beast will not enter Israel until the second beast has paved the way. He will be like Elijah, and is called the false prophet (Revelation 19:20). The destiny of both beasts is the same. They will be tossed alive into the lake of fire (Revelation 19:20).

The Jehovah's Witnesses.

When the Holy Spirit descended on Pentecost, there was a sudden sound from heaven like a mighty rushing wind. The sound filled the house where the disciples of one accord had been sitting. Cloven tongues like flames appeared upon each one of them, they were filled with the Holy Spirit of God and they began to speak in sundry languages as the Spirit gave them utterance.

Because of the Feast of Weeks, many devout Jewish people were dwelling in the city of Jerusalem from every populated nation. When the phenomenon became known, multitudes of these devoted Jewish pilgrims came together and they were astonished because every man heard the Spirit-filled believers speaking in the native language of the lands from which they had journeyed.

This unprecedented phenomenon changed the world more than any other single event in man's history. The world had been invaded by a supernatural force that has been steadily conquering one life at time from that time forward until now. The Jehovah's witnesses had been empowered, commissioned and released upon the pagan planet and nothing has been the same since. We have no statistics as to the number of souls that were saved on that day, but as spectacular as that marvelous occurrence was, it pales in comparison to the end time revival of the great tribulation.

At Pentecost, the number of witnesses were about one hundred and twenty people (Acts 1:15). That might be larger than most Messianic congregations, but it was still only one hundred and twenty. In the Great Tribulation the number of witnessing people will be one hundred and forty four thousand. Over one thousand times more people; that should multiply the impact.

In Acts, the witnesses were of one accord, were Spirit filled and were highly motivated. The end times Jehovah witnesses are described as virgins, who had not been defiled with women and who follow the lamb. They are called the first fruits of God, showing that they will reproduce a harvest, there is no guile in their mouths and they stand blameless before the throne (Revelation 14:4-5).

Immediately following the sealing of the 144,000, we read about an uncountable multitude. In the book of Acts, at the first movement of the Holy Spirit, only Jewish people responded to the Gospel. Now it is true that those Jewish people were mostly travelers who certainly impacted their native lands upon their return. But the likelihood is that mostly, if not only, Jewish people were impacted. In Revelation we read about a great multitude, that no man could number, that included representatives, from every nation, kindred, peoples and language groups. Certainly this describes the greatest response to the gospel in all of history.

There are some questions as to the identification of the 144,000. There are various lists of the tribes in the Old Testament (Genesis 35:22-26; 46:8-27; 49:1-27, Exodus 1:1-5; Numbers 1:5-13; 13:4; 26:1-65; Deuteronomy 27:11-13; 33:6-24; Joshua 13-22, Judges 5, 1 Chronicles 2-8; 12:24-37; 27:16-22;Ezekiel 48) and given in various orders. Jacob had twelve sons; however, Joseph receives a double portion in that each of his two sons is included. All the lists total twelve tribes, but they include and exclude different sons to keep the number at twelve. In 1 Chronicles 7:12 both Dan and Zebulon are omitted. The 144,000 are called out from the tribes of Israel, but the tribe of Dan is not mentioned and Manasses is.[13] Manasses is the son of Joseph and, since Joseph is also mentioned, it is difficult to understand why they both would appear; and yet the other son of Joseph (Ephraim) is not mentioned. If the tribes were referring to geographical territory in the restored nation of Israel then it would be unusual to see Levi mentioned since his portion was cities within the other tribal territories.

It appears that the tribes are referring to actual family connections. Some would question how family connection could be restored after all these centuries when none has been maintained. The Jewish people have not married within tribes and have not kept tribal distinctions. For the most part, only the tribe of Judah and the tribe of Levi are ever known.

The Rabbis establish a person's Jewish identity on the basis of the mother. If your mom is Jewish, you are Jewish. However, your father determines your tribe. If your father is a Levi, you are a Levi. Now, it can get confusing in a mixed marriage between a Jew and a Gentile. A Jewish woman who marries a Gentile man will have Jewish children, who will have no tribal identity. Conversely, a Jewish man, from the tribe of Judah, who marries a Gentile woman will have children that have a tribal connection to the tribe of Judah, but they would not be

Jewish. However, if the connection to the original tribes is maintained through the father, there is a line that can be traced back to Biblical times, a line that remains unbroken regardless of how many Gentile moms have been added in.

> *" And I heard the number of them which were sealed: [and there were] sealed an hundred [and] forty [and] four thousand of all the tribes of the children of Israel. Of the tribe of Juda [were] sealed twelve thousand. Of the tribe of Reuben [were] sealed twelve thousand. Of the tribe of Gad [were] sealed twelve thousand. Of the tribe of Aser [were] sealed twelve thousand. Of the tribe of Nepthalim [were] sealed twelve thousand. Of the tribe of Manasses [were] sealed twelve thousand .Of the tribe of Simeon [were] sealed twelve thousand. Of the tribe of Levi [were] sealed twelve thousand. Of the tribe of Issachar [were] sealed twelve thousand. Of the tribe of Zabulon [were] sealed twelve thousand. Of the tribe of Joseph [were] sealed twelve thousand. Of the tribe of Benjamin [were] sealed twelve thousand.* Revelation 7:4-8

Rachel	Leah	Bilhah	Zilpah
11. Joseph	1. Reuben	5. Dan	7. Gad
12. Benjamin	2. Simeon	6. Naphtali	8. Asher
	3. Levi		
	4. Judah		
	9. Issachar		
	10. Zebulon		

The first 12,000 come from the tribe of Judah. It is not unusual to see Judah, the fourth son, being mentioned first, because of the messianic line. Reuben is coupled with Judah and after that each son is mentioned as we move across the chart, from right to left, with his own brother in couplets. Except, where you would expect to read "Dan", "Manasses" has been slipped in. There is a very unreliable text that reads "Dan" in the place where our much more dependable text reads "Manasses".

That text is so spurious that it would have to be considered inadmissible evidence. A good lawyer and a good judge would never allow the jury to even hear the information, and if you did hear it you would be sternly instructed to disregard it. Well, I am neither an attorney nor a judge and in my world of questionable scholarship, I will mention it in an attempt to at least get a mistrial in the case for the tribe of Dan.

These 144,000 are sealed on their foreheads with the name of God (Revelation 7:3,14:1). The seal is to protect them in Revelation 7, but by the time we reach Revelation 14 they have all been redeemed from the earth (Revelation 14:3), and stand before the throne (Revelation 14:5). We are not told exactly how they die. I suppose that they are eventually martyred. I have no idea why the Lord first seals them, and then allows them to be killed. In the time of their lives, they prove themselves to be the most effective evangelistic force ever.

There are far more than 144,000 believers on the planet today. We are all filled with the same power that invaded the world on the day of Pentecost; however, we are not producing a harvest of any significance. Could it be that we are not following the lamb (Revelation 14:4), or perhaps some of us cannot be described by the phrase *"they loved not their lives unto the death"* (Revelation 12:11).

The Judgments

Before the angels are allowed to hurt the earth, the 144,000 are sealed for protection. Then the trumpet and the vial judgments begin. Most of the commentaries see the trumpet judgments as the beginning of the Tribulation and see the vial judgments as being more intense and occurring in the second three and a half years.

It is possible that both the trumpet and vial judgments are describing the same events from two different perspectives. The trumpet judgments view the entire globe and describe the judgments as occurring on $1/3^{rd}$ of the globe in the Middle East. The vial judgments view the world as the old Roman world and describe the same judgments as affecting the whole earth, or rather the whole Roman world. When we look at the judgments in that light, the trumpet and vials compliment each other, as they define and explain each other.

"The first angel sounded and there followed hail and fire mingled with blood and they were cast upon the earth: and the third part of trees was burnt up and all green grass was burnt up." Revelation 8:7

"And the first went and poured out his vial upon the earth; and there fell a noisome and grievous sore upon the men which had the mark of the beast and (upon) them which worshipped his image." Revelation 16:2

The first trumpet speaks of hail mingled with blood and fire. The hail and fire were mingled with blood and then cast upon the earth. It is not hard to imagine a hailstorm, accompanied by lightening. The mention of fire and blood is hard to understand. Perhaps the lightening causes the fires and they destroy the fruit trees and vegetation, while hail falling on men result in the blood.

Hail is always used for judgment in the Scriptures. When the king of Assyria was poised to pounce on Samaria, God referred to him as a *"tempest of hail and a destroying storm"*, Isaiah 28:2.[14] This end time judgment of hail was mentioned in the book of Job, *"hast thou seen the treasures of the hail, which I have reserved against the time of trouble, against the day of battle and war?"* (Job 38:22-3).

The language of the first trumpet is not dissimilar to what we see during the plagues on Egypt in Exodus 9:23-25. Also, the first bowl speaks of grievous sores upon men. The language of the second bowl judgment is similar to the plague described in Exodus 9:8-11. The hailstorm would easily produce the sores. The first bowl mentions that the sores come only upon the men who have received the mark of the beast. The Jewish beast causes his fellow Jewish people to receive the mark, threatening them with death. Those who capitulate and receive the mark will suffer from the grievous sores from the hailstorm.

Are We There Yet?

These severe and painful sores do not seem to disappear as we read in Revelation 16:10-11. Yet for all of the suffering, men refuse to repent and continue to blaspheme the God of all glory. The heart of man is truly deceitful and desperately wicked. It is frightening to think that the same rebellious, pernicious heart is at the seat of our thoughts and emotions.

> *"And the second angel sounded, and as it were a great mountain burning with fire was cast into the sea: and the third part of the sea became blood; And the third part of the creatures which were in the sea, and had life, died; and the third part of the ships were destroyed."* Revelation 8:8-9

> *"And the second angel poured out his vial upon the sea; and it became as the blood of a dead (man): and every living soul died in the sea."* Revelation 16:3

The second trumpet judgment begins with the phrase, *"as it were a great mountain burning with fire"*. There is no literal mountain. Perhaps a vast meteor will fall into the Mediterranean Sea and everything in that sea will be destroyed. The second bowl refers to all the souls in the sea dying. The Old Testament frequently refers to animals and fish as souls (Genesis 1:21,24; 2:19; 9:10, 12).[15] So both the second bowl and the second trumpet describe death to all the fish and destruction of all the ships in the Mediterranean Sea.

> *"And the third angel sounded and there fell a great star from heaven, burning as it were a lamp and it fell upon the third part of the rivers and upon the fountains of waters; And the name of the star is called Wormwood: and the third part of the waters became wormwood; and many men died of the waters, because they were made bitter."* Revelation 8:10-11

> *"And the third angel poured out his vial upon the rivers and fountains of waters; and they became blood. And I heard the angel of the waters say, Thou art righteous, O Lord, which art and wast and shalt be, because thou hast judged thus. For they have shed the blood of saints and prophets and thou hast given them blood to drink; for they are worthy. And I heard another out of the altar say,*

Even so, Lord God Almighty, true and righteous are thy judgments" Revelation 16:4-7

The third judgment focuses on the fresh water, rivers, lakes and streams of the Middle East. The rivers becoming blood parallels the first of the Egyptian plagues. The bowl judgment does not describe how the waters became blood, but justifies the action on the basis of the fact that these people have shed the blood of saints so they will now be left with only blood to drink.

The inhabitants of the earth could be held accountable for the shedding of the blood of the saints if they just stood by and refused to help or get involved. However from Matthew 24:9, it appears that they are far more culpable than just not helping. They are actually so filled with hatred for God that violent mobs and vicious gangs repeatedly seek out and kill the saints, with certain blessings from the world ruler. The third trumpet describes a meteor falling upon the fresh waters of the Middle East causing them to become bitter. In Ezekiel 47:9 we read about the healing of the waters.

"And the fourth angel sounded and the third part of the sun was smitten and the third part of the moon and the third part of the stars; so as the third part of them was darkened and the day shone not for a third part of it and the night likewise." Revelation 8:12

"And the fourth angel poured out his vial upon the sun; and power was given unto him to scorch men with fire. And men were scorched with great heat and blasphemed the name of God, which hath power over these plagues: and they repented not to give him glory." Revelation 16:8-9

These cataclysmic events described in the fourth judgment are mentioned in several previous texts. Ezekiel 32:7 speaks about the covering of darkness in the heavens as the stars and the sun are covered and the moon fails to give light. In Matthew 24 the stars are said to fall from heaven at the end of the tribulation and at that time the sun and moon fail to give their light. Matthew describes these events occurring at the end of the tribulation, while the fourth trumpet and bowl judgments predict three more judgments will happen before the tribulation ends. It is possible that the celestial abnormalities continue until the end of the tribulation.

The darkness covers the earth yet great heat scorches the inhabitants of the earth. I always associated the heat and light energies together but in this strange judgment the light is removed and the heat is intensified to unbearable proportions and yet the Jewish people will not repent.

> *"And I beheld and heard an angel flying through the midst of heaven, saying with a loud voice, Woe, woe, woe, to the inhabitants of the earth by reason of the other voices of the trumpet of the three angels which are yet to sound!"* Revelation 8:13

After the fourth trumpet an angel flies across the skies announcing the horrors that await the inhabitants of planet earth in the following three judgments. As bad as the plagues have been, things are now going to grow severely worse, as we pass into the second half of Daniel's 70th week.

> *"And the fifth angel sounded and I saw a star fall from heaven unto the earth: and to him was given the key of the bottomless pit. And he opened the bottomless pit; and there arose a smoke out of the pit, as the smoke of a great furnace; and the sun and the air were darkened by reason of the smoke of the pit. And there came out of the smoke locusts upon the earth: and unto them was given power, as the scorpions of the earth have power. And it was commanded them that they should not hurt the grass of the earth, neither any green thing, neither any tree; but only those men which have not the seal of God in their foreheads. And to them it was given that they should not kill them, but that they should be tormented five months: and their torment was as the torment of a scorpion, when he striketh a man. And in those days shall men seek death and shall not find it; and shall desire to die and death shall flee from them. And the shapes of the locusts were like unto horses prepared unto battle; and on their heads were as it were crowns like gold and their faces were as the faces of men. And they had hair as the hair*

of women and their teeth were as the teeth of lions. And they had breastplates, as it were breastplates of iron; and the sound of their wings was as the sound of chariots of many horses running to battle. And they had tails like unto scorpions and there were stings in their tails: and their power was to hurt men five months. And they had a king over them, which is the angel of the bottomless pit, whose name in the Hebrew tongue is Abaddon, but in the Greek tongue hath his name Apollyon One woe is past; and, behold, there come two woes more hereafter." Revelation 9:1-12

"And the fifth angel poured out his vial upon the seat of the beast; and his kingdom was full of darkness; and they gnawed their tongues for pain and blasphemed the God of heaven because of their pains and their sores and repented not of their deeds". Revelation 16:10-11

The fifth bowl describes men in excruciating agony, but it does not tell us what is causing the pain. However, the fifth trumpet describes the source of their extreme discomfort at length. Demons are released from the pit, but they are not allowed to harm the vegetation. They are assigned to torture men, but are not allowed to harm the 144,000 Jehovah's witnesses who have received the seal of God. And the demons are not allowed to kill men, but are sent to torture for five months the Jewish people who have not repented. These demons are some of Satan's most vicious, evil followers.

When Jesus cast the demons out of the maniac of Gadara, the demons expressed their strong reluctance to be assigned to the pit.[16] In both Jude 6 and II Peter 2:4 we read about this confining pit for the fallen angels. In both passages, the pit is seen as an example of the extreme justice and severity of the judgment of God. These demonic beings are described as wearing long hair and iron-like breastplates; they have teeth like lions, tails like scorpions and in flight, their wings sound like an army of chariots drawn by horses. They are frightening in appearance, deafening in their reverberation and incalculably horrid in their directive. As bad as their bark might be, it is quite apparent that their bite will far exceed it.

Are We There Yet?

The demons had been confined in a place of torture for centuries and they are now released. Filled with anguish and hatred they are now set free to torment the people of the earth for five months. It is no wonder that the angel pronounces woes upon the inhabitants of the earth. And yet, for all of that horror, we learn that man will continue to blaspheme God and refuse to repent of their deeds.

Every trial can turn us. A difficulty can drive us to our knees, to cause us to call upon the name of the Lord, or we can use the trial as an excuse to abandon our faith and to find reason to curse. The intensity of the trial can result in a more intense commitment or a more intense rebellion. The desperately wicked heart of man chooses to continue in defiant rebellion.

> *"And the sixth angel sounded and I heard a voice from the four horns of the golden altar which is before God, Saying to the sixth angel which had the trumpet, Loose the four angels which are bound in the great river Euphrates. And the four angels were loosed, which were prepared for an hour and a day and a month and a year, for to slay the third part of men. And the number of the army of the horsemen were two hundred thousand thousand: and I heard the number of them. And thus I saw the horses in the vision and them that sat on them, having breastplates of fire and of jacinth and brimstone: and the heads of the horses were as the heads of lions; and out of their mouths issued fire and smoke and brimstone. By these three was the third part of men killed, by the fire and by the smoke and by the brimstone, which issued out of their mouths. For their power is in their mouth and in their tails: for their tails were like unto serpents and had heads and with them they do hurt. And the rest of the men which were not killed by these plagues yet repented not of the works of their hands, that they should not worship devils and idols of gold and silver and brass and stone and of wood: which neither can see, nor hear, nor walk: Neither repented they of their murders, nor of their sorceries, nor of their fornication, nor of their thefts."* Revelation 9:12-21

> *"And the sixth angel poured out his vial upon the great river Euphrates; and the water thereof was dried up, that the way of the*

> *kings of the east might be prepared. And I saw three unclean spirits like frogs come out of the mouth of the dragon and out of the mouth of the beast and out of the mouth of the false prophet. For they are the spirits of devils, working miracles, which go forth unto the kings of the earth and of the whole world, to gather them to the battle of that great day of God Almighty. Behold, I come as a thief. Blessed is he that watcheth and keepeth his garments, lest he walk naked and they see his shame. And he gathered them together into a place called in the Hebrew tongue Armageddon."* Revelation 16:12-16

In both the sixth trumpet and the sixth bowl we see the river Euphrates dried up. Then a 200,000,000 man army marches across the dried up river in preparation for the Armageddon campaign. The army of men in the bowl judgment is infused by demons. The demons are described in the trumpet judgment. The military destroys 1/3 of the Jewish people and the demons destroy a second third by fire, smoke and brimstone, which proceed out of their mouths.

Two thirds of the Jewish people who stay in the land and do not heed the warning of Jesus to flee given in Matthew 24:16-20 are destroyed as we read in Zechariah 13:8. The one third that is left are driven to take refuge in the city of Jerusalem, where the united armies of the world surround them, siege the city and eventually overtake it.

> *"And the seventh angel sounded; and there were great voices in heaven, saying, The kingdoms of this world are become (the kingdoms) of our Lord and of his Christ; and he shall reign for ever and ever. And the four and twenty elders, which sat before God on their seats, fell upon their faces and worshiped God, Saying We give thee thanks, O Lord God Almighty, which art and wast and art to come; because thou hast taken to thee thy great power and hast reigned. And the nations were angry and thy wrath is come, and the time of the dead, that they should be judged, and that thou shouldest give reward unto to thy servants the prophets, and to the saints, andthem that fear your name, small and great; and shouldest destroy them which destroy the earth. And the temple of God was opened in heaven, and there was seen in his temple the*

> *ark of his testament; and there were lightnings, and voices, and thunderings, and an earthquak,e and great hail."* Revelation 11:15-19

> *"And the seventh angel poured out his vial into the air; and there came a great voice out of the temple of heaven, from the throne, saying, It is done. And there were voices, and thunders, and lightnings; and there was a great earthquake, such as was not since men were upon the earth, so mighty an earthquake (and) so great. And the great city was divided into three parts, and the cities of the nations fell: and great Babylon came in remembrance before God, to give unto her the cup of the wine of the fierceness of his wrath. And every island fled away and the mountains were not found. And there fell upon men a great hail out of heaven, (every ston)e about the weight of a talent: and men blasphemed God because of the plague of the hail; for the plague thereof was exceeding great."* Revelation 16:17-21

The seventh judgment brings us to the end of the tribulation. In the trumpet judgment the world's kingdoms are finally delivered over to the Lord and the righteous dead receive their long-awaited award. In the seventh bowl, a great voice cries out from the temple declaring, *"it is done."* In the seventh bowl, the city of Babylon falls under the wrath of God. Both descriptions mention the great earthquake. The bowl report shows how the earthquake divides the city of Jerusalem, which according to Zechariah 14:4, provides the way of escape for the Jewish remnant.

The Law and The Prophets

In Revelation 11, we read about two witnesses. These two witnesses are not angels, nations nor churches; they are finite men. Satan himself will kill them and let their dead bodies lie in the street for the whole world to see. Because they both die, many people think that these two witnesses must be Enoch and Elijah, the only two men who did not die.

I understand that it is appointed for man to die once (Hebrews 9:27), which is the overwhelming truth regarding the history of man. All men die. However, when the rapture occurs, those who are caught up alive to be with the Lord will escape death; an entire generation that does not die.

Enoch is a picture of that generation. Enoch walked with God and before the judgment of the great flood, God took Enoch alive into heaven (Genesis 5:18), just like He will take the believers alive into heaven before the judgment of the great tribulation (1 Thessalonians 4:17).

We know that one of the two men is Elijah. There can be no doubt about this fact. The Scriptures declare that God will send Elijah the prophet before the great and dreadful day of the Lord (Malachi 4:5). When Malachi identified Elijah, he also gave us a clue regarding the identity of the other witness.

In Malachi 4:4, the Jewish people are admonished to remember the law of Moses. Jesus explains to the disciples in the Sermon on the Mount how he did not come to destroy the law and the prophets. When Jesus spoke of the law and the prophets, he was referring to the witness of the Scriptures. He tells the unbelieving Jewish leaders in John's gospel to search the Scriptures, because the Scriptures testify of Him (John 5:39). On the road to Emmaus, after the resurrection, Jesus shows the two travelers all that the Scriptures said in regards to Him.

> *"And beginning at Moses and all the prophets, he expounded unto them in all the scriptures the things concerning himself."* Luke 24:27

The Law and the Prophets are the two witnesses of the Messiah. The Law is the law of Moses, and the Prophets are represented by the most outstanding prophet, Elijah. The two witnesses are referred to as the two olive trees and the two candlesticks standing before God in Revelation 11:4. This reference takes us back to Zechariah 4 where the olive trees are called the two anointed ones. Those who are the anointed ones of the Scriptures are prophets, priests and kings.

It is my opinion that these two anointed witnesses are both prophets. When we think of Moses we think of the law. Few of us think of Moses as a prophet, however, we know that he is (Deuteronomy 18:15). The Jews require a sign and together these two provide the encouraging signs that fulfill the requirements of rebelling Israel. They have the power that Elijah did to shut up the heavens so that it does not rain as during his earthly ministry, and to turn rivers into blood and smite the earth with plagues as Moses did during his earthly ministry.

According to one of my all time favorite Bible teachers, Dr. Clarence Mason, these two witnesses have a history of working together. In Matthew 17, at what has become known as the Mount of Transfiguration, Moses and Elijah appear alongside of Jesus. In that event, the Law and the Prophets testified by their presence, to the small group of apostles, regarding the preeminence of Jesus. Peter wanted to erect three temporary dwellings, one for each of the prominent persons, Elijah, Moses and Jesus. The Father voiced His opinion from heaven out of a cloud as He proclaimed *"this is my beloved Son, in whom I am well pleased."*

At the tomb, on the morning of the resurrection, there were two messengers present.[17] Is it possible that Moses and Elijah, the law and the prophets, are announcing the fact of the glorious resurrection? Dr. Mason suggested that the law and the prophets predicted Israel's Messiah, declared His uniqueness, testified of His resurrection and were present again at the ascension. Who would be better than the law and the prophets, the dynamic duo, at announcing to the early Jewish church that the same Messiah who disappeared into the clouds from the Mount of Olives will return in the same manner? (Acts 1:10-11)

CHAPTER SIX

The Great White Throne

When all the great plants of our cities have ceased from all of their work,
When the merchant has sold the last yard of silk,
    and dismissed the last tired clerk.
When the bank has raked in the last dollar,
    and paid out the last dividend,
When the judge of the earth says, closed for the night,
    and asks for a balance, What then?
When the projector has shown the last picture,
    and the scoreboard flashed the last run
When the actor recites his last soliloquy,
    and the comedian his final pun,
When the crowd seeking pleasure go out into the night,
    and into the darkness again,
When the King of the earth sits on the great throne
    and the dead stand in His sight, What then?
When the Choir has sang the last chorus,
    and the preacher has said the last prayer
When the people have heard the last sermon,
    and the sound has died out in the air,
When the Bible is closed on the lectern,
    and the pews are all empty of men.
When the small and the great face their record,
    and stand before him, What then?

                              Author Unknown

Are We There Yet?

I love the bumper sticker that reads, "prepare for your finals, read the Bible." During my first stint in college I remember a folk song that repeated the line "O sinner man where you gonna run to in that day." The Serendipity Singers trivialized a universal and awesome concept. The prospect of a supreme and ultimate final exam must be intimidating.

I hate all examinations; I love darkness rather than light because my deeds are evil (John 3:19). I am so frightened of the process of examination and possible illumination, that I do not even relish administering exams. Judgment day might be intimidating, but it is a fact. If we do not accept the Savior, we will have to face the Judge. The Apostle John describes the inevitable and awesome day in five succinct verses. It is like a reporter jotting down a brief outline, as John records for us who, what, when, where and how of the "Great White Throne"!

Who (is on the throne?)

John saw a Great White Throne and Him whom was enthroned upon it. We know Jesus, the Son of God, is on the throne. There can be no doubt about that. In the gospel of John we read how the Father does not judge anyone and He will not judge anyone, because He has committed all judgment to the Son (John 5:22).

The same word for judge is translated "condemn" in John 3:17, where we read how the Father did not send His son into the world to condemn (or judge) the world. How are we to explain the seeming contradiction? God did not send His son to judge, yet God has committed all judgment over to the Son? It is all rather simple. John 3:17 is a purpose clause. It was not the intent of God for Jesus to judge the world; the purpose was that through Jesus the world might be saved. However, those who do not come to the Savior will have to face the Judge.

The Great White Throne

Jesus is the hanging judge of all eternity. When I was in my late teens, a car got stolen. Notice the use of the passive voice. It was not like *we* stole the car; it was more the activity of the car. That occurred some forty years ago and I really do not recall the details, although I do remember a bit of the emotions. I remember how frightening the process of the criminal justice system loomed up to be. The judge had extreme powers regarding the dispensation of our lives. The judge could, because of our youthfulness, find mitigation in the circumstance of our first offence and dismiss the charges. Or the judge could find us guilty of grand theft auto and assign to us a whole plethora of fines and penalties. The judge could fine us thousands of dollars and ruin any chance of going to college. If we got jobs to pay off the fines we would become eligible for the draft. In those days the only way to avoid the draft was to stay in school. The judge could send us to the county farm, a detention center for juvenile delinquents. A pleasant stay there is usually for six months to two years of hard labor. The judge could send us to Kankakee jail for a longer term.

There was a lady judge who had a reputation for her harsh decisions. She had no patience for teens and no mercy for first timers. She was known as, what was affectionately referred to as a hanging judge, a judge who was tough on crime, a judge who took the task of upholding justice seriously.

Today, I would applaud such a judge. Forty years ago the last thing I needed was that lady judge hearing our case. Every time her name appeared on the docket, our attorney would get a postponement, hoping that we could get a different judge assigned to us. After awhile it became obvious she was looking for us, she wanted our case in her courtroom. If I remember correctly, our hearing finally arrived on a Friday morning. Now here's the truly wonderful part of it all. On Wednesday night a nincompoop went out and stole the judge's car.

Can you imagine? We had to stand trial before a judge who had a reputation for being tough on juvenile delinquents, crime and first time offenders. We had to face a judge who hated car thieves and we were

Are We There Yet?

juvenile delinquents, first time offender car thieves. Just to make it really interesting, the judge had to take two busses and a train to get to work that morning because some fool had stolen the judge's car.

Now having related this incident on a score of occasions over the past thirty-five years, I have learned that everyone wants to know the outcome of my escapade. I would love to try to hide from the embarrassment of those years before I knew the Lord, or about obeying Biblical principles. The fact is that there was some technicality and we were released. However, even though I did not have to pay for the crime, I specifically remember the fear of facing the judge. We all tried to look cool, but inside our emotions were churning as we were fighting back tears and when we discovered the news about the judge's car, we just knew we were doomed.

Jesus is the hanging judge of all eternity. We know it is Jesus who sits on the throne from the Scriptures. The Scriptures also teach us that all our crimes were perpetrated against Him personally (Psalm 51:4). If you will allow an analogy from my own past, we stole the car that belongs to Jesus. Jesus is the hanging judge of all eternity because He bore the sin, he paid the penalty for the sin in His own body (I Peter 2:24). Following through with our analogy, Jesus went to the county farm and did the two years hard labor for us. The crime was against Him, and the penalty was paid by Him. Some refuse to accept the pardon, some will insist on having their day in court, they refuse to accept mercy, they want to face the judge. Let us suggest that the judge they face will be the Lord Jesus, the hanging judge of all eternity.

Who (is before the throne?)

Before the throne the dead are gathered, both small and great. The expression small and great shows us that this judgment is universal. The dead come from three places, sea, death and hell. Daniel helps us identify who these three groups might be.

The Great White Throne

"And there shall be a time of trouble, such as never was since there was a nation even to that same time:" Daniel 12:1

Before the nation of Israel was called into existence through the patriarchs Abraham, Isaac and Jacob, the unbelievers of the world were destroyed through the great flood. It would not be unusual to expect that they would be reserved in the sea until the Day of Judgment. From the time of the nation of Israel forward, the unbelievers were kept in what the Scriptures call death, and during the Church age the unbelievers are sent to hell to await the resurrection before the great white throne.

Those who stand before the throne experience what the Scriptures refer to as the "second death" (Revelation 20:14). There are two destinies that face all of mankind; the second death and the First Resurrection (Revelation 20:6). The first resurrection is a battalion of believers that exists in five companies. Company "A" is the Lord Jesus, the first fruits, and after that company "B"; they who are Christ's at His coming (1 Corinthians 15:23).

After the resurrection of the believers of the Church age the Great Tribulation begins. In the middle of that Tribulation the two witnesses are slain and then raised for the whole world to see. These two witnesses constitute company "C" (Revelation 11:9-11).

After the Tribulation, the Old Testament saints and those who died during the Great Tribulation are raised, (Daniel 12:2), describes the resurrection of company "D". There will be death in the millennium. Those believers who die during the kingdom need to receive their spiritual bodies that will last for eternity so the rest of the dead live not until the thousand years are finished (Revelation 20:5). Therefore, Company "E" consists of those believers who die during the kingdom and are raised at its completion.

"Marvel not at this: for the hour is coming, in the which all that are in the graves shall hear his voice and shall come forth; they

that have done good, unto the resurrection of life: and they that have done evil, unto the resurrection of damnation." John 5:28-9

John's gospel speaks about the resurrection. John contrasts the experience of the raised believers with the experience of the unbeliever. Notice in John the contrast is not between life and death. The contrast is between life and judgment. The unbelieving dead do not face annihilation, but are raised for judgment.

"And many of them that sleep in the dust of the earth shall awake, some to everlasting life and some to shame and everlasting contempt." Daniel 12:2

In Daniel we are also introduced to the resurrection of the dead. In both passages we see believers and unbelievers being raised and there is a contrast between the resurrection of the believers and the resurrection of the unbelievers. In both passages the believers are raised to life. In John's gospel the believer is raised to life while the unbeliever is raised to judgment. In Daniel the unbeliever is raised to shame and then to everlasting contempt, both of which are the results of judgment.

In both Daniel and John the believer is raised first. In Daniel all the dead are not raised. This is a partial resurrection of Old Testament saints and tribulation martyrs. The language of Daniel 12 shows a gap of time between the two resurrections. We know that gap is a gap of 1,000 years between the resurrection of believing Israel at the end of the tribulation and the resurrection of the unbelievers at the end of the kingdom.

At the resurrection of believers of each of the companies, there are those who were left behind. As the believers are raised to life, the unbelievers are left to wait for judgment day. The result of judgment day is shame and everlasting contempt.

On the throne is Jesus, the hanging judge of all eternity. Before the throne is a crowd of unbelievers, small and great, from every age of man's sad and sorry history. Men, who mocked and disregarded the

The Great White Throne

warnings of Noah, will stay in the sea and wait for the judgment. Those who refused to believe in Abraham's God will be raised to stand alongside the Egyptian pharaoh, who hardened his heart at the time of Moses. Those who mocked the Jewish people form the walls of Jericho and the Kings of Israel, who did wickedly in unbelief, will stand before the throne. Those who persecuted the Jewish people in Persia under Haman, in Syria under Antiochus and in Rome under Nero, will all stand before the throne. People who rejected the resurrection of Jesus and the Gospel of Paul plus the people who reject the Gospel as you preach it by lip and proclaim it by life, will all be raised at the end of kingdom, to stand before the judge.

When?

When the Great White Throne takes place is the simplest of the facts about the Great White Throne to discern. Revelation 20:7 states that the thousand years have been completed. Revelation 21:1 tells us that John sees a new heaven and new earth. The events of the Great White Throne take place between the two verses; after the kingdom is completed and before the new heavens and the new earth, so don't worry about it you won't be late.

Where?

In contrast to the *time* of the Great White Throne, the *place* of the Great White Throne is rather complicated to discern. However, there is a blessing if we are willing to do the study it takes discover what the Scriptures are teaching. Both Revelation 21:1 and II Peter 3:13 speak about new heavens and a new earth.

> *"And I saw a new heaven and a new earth: for the first heaven and the first earth were passed away; and there was no more sea."*
> Revelation 21:1

> *"Nevertheless we, according to his promise, look for new heavens and a new earth, wherein dwelleth righteousness."* II Peter 3:13

Revelation teaches us that the first heavens and earth passed away. The passage offers little explanation as to what *"passed away"* means. II Peter 3 tells us that the heavens will pass away with a fervent heat. And then continues to describe a loud noise and how the earth and the heavens are burned up.

> *"But the day of the Lord will come as a thief in the night; in the which the heavens shall pass away with a great noise and the elements shall melt with fervent heat, the earth also and the works that are therein shall be burned up."* II Peter 3:12

The language of II Peter 3 has been misunderstood to describe some kind of nuclear disaster. This interpretation was a common theme during the years of the Cuban missile crisis and the cold war with the former Soviet Union. I remember one preacher on television reading from the headlines and then quoting II Peter to show we are about to blow ourselves off the face of the earth and it was all predicted in the Word of God. The truly amazing thing is that this preacher is still on television and still reading the newspaper then going to the concordance to find Bible verses that say similar things and Christians are still watching, listening and believing.

It is certain that the earth will melt from a fervent heat. The heavens will be on fire and dissolve, which is the fate of the old heavens and earth; the earth that we now live in. Seeing that these things must be dissolved, we are admonished to live lives with all holy conversation and godliness as in the verses 13 and 14. The Bible is not teaching us that we are going to blow ourselves off the planet. If it were, we would be urged to study nuclear physics rather than godly living. The blast, the heat and the fire have to do with the character of God.

Revelation directly relates the fate of the heavens and earth to the person who sits on the great white throne.

> *"And I saw a great white throne and him that sat on it, from whose face the earth and the heaven fled away; and there was found no place for them"* Revelation 20:11

The Great White Throne

Revelation makes it clear that the heavens and earth fled away from the face of the one sitting on the throne and there was no place left for them. It seems that the face of Jesus is so brilliant that the heat that comes from the bright light of His glory causes the time/space universe to melt in His glorious presence. Now, that description should urge us on to godliness. The meek and lowly Jesus is the mighty, glorious, everlasting God.

Where does the great white throne happen? Well the heavens and earth had passed away. And the new heavens and new earth are yet future, the great white throne takes place in the no place. There is a spatial warp of some kind in which the great white throne is established.

What?

According to Revelation 20, in the process of the examination, the books are opened and the book of life is opened also. The dead were judged according to their works out of the things written in the books. Apparently the works of men are being recorded for future judgment. Since all those standing before the judge lost their case, the book of life is consulted. When their names are not found in the book of life, they are cast into the lake of fire, which is the second death (Revelation 20:12,15).

In Exodus 32:32, Moses is willing to sacrifice himself to appease the wrath of God for the sake of the nation of Israel. He asks to be blotted out of the book, which God had written. The language seems to indicate that everyone born is written in the book. Everyone has potential eternal life. In Exodus 32:33, we read how people will have their names blotted out of the book. In Psalms 69:28 and 109:13 we read about people who have their names blotted out of the book and their names will not be written with the righteous.[1]

According to Psalms, the names of those who have been declared righteous are written at some later time. In addition to the books which record the works of men, there appears to be two additional books. Both are called the book of life, however, one is more accurately translated as "the Lambs scroll of eternal life."[2]

Everyone born is recorded in the book of life, because everyone has potential life in the federal headship of Jesus (1 Corinthians 15:22). Those who die in unbelief will be blotted out of that book. A selected few, who live lives of such exaggerated evil, might accomplish the goal of being blotted out while they are still alive. Once blotted out, your name will never be written with the names of those who have been declared righteous in the Scroll of eternal life (Psalm 69:28, 109:13). If during a lifetime an individual chooses to place faith in the sacrifice of Jesus, then that person's name is immediately and indelibly inscribed in the Lamb's scroll of eternal life, never to be removed.

We know from Isaiah 45:23 that every knee shall bend and that every tongue shall vow allegiance. This is repeated in the New Testament in Romans 14:11 and Philippians 2:10 In the Romans passage, it is referring to the believers who stand before the judgment seat of Christ.[3]

What happens at the Great White Throne is this. The unbelievers, small and great, stand before the throne and their works are examined. When their works show that they have not earned them entrance into eternal life, the book of life is referred to. Those standing before the throne will drop to their knees. They will confess that Jesus is Lord to the glory of God the Father and they will say the very words they had avoided, shunned and hated all their lives. The very words, had they been spoken by faith, would have resulted in eternal life but are now spoken by sight. The confession is too late and their names are not found written in the book of the righteous so they are cast into the outer darkness, which is the second death (Revelation 20:15).[4] How lonely will solitary confinement be after being in the presence of the God who is love? How dark will the outer darkness be?

How?

The unbelieving dead, small and great, from every age of man's history, are raised to stand before the Great White Throne. They are judged on the basis of their works (Revelation 20:12,13). The text repeats the basis of the judgment. Twice we read the phrase "according to their works". They are not judged on the basis of their sins, because Jesus Christ was the propitiation for their sins (1 John 2:2). They are not judged on the basis of their faith because we are saved by faith. If they had faith they would have been raised in the first resurrection. They refused to accept the mercy of God, rejected the salvation of God and now the justice of God will examine their works. They will be judged on the basis of their works.

I suppose human works could be seen in two categories. We could look at religious works and we could look at basic human, non-religious, good deeds. It is in regard to religious accomplishments that Paul writes in Philippians. There he relates his Jewish pedigree. He tells us about his circumcision on the eight-day, according to the accepted ritual. He mentions he is from the tribe of Benjamin, and he tells us he is a Hebrew of the Hebrews. Those things relate to the way the Apostle was born. Then he begins to describe the things he had done religiously in the flesh. He was a zealous Pharisee and he persecuted what he thought was a false religious cult. Paul concludes this section by saying that in touching the righteousness of the law, he is blameless. Paul kept the Torah, yet when comparing his religious pedigree to the knowledge of Christ, he sums the good works up as refuse. The word he used for refuse is skubalon. It often refers to dung.

When we show Jewish people the gospel in the Old Testament, we always begin with several verses that show the bad news. We show them Scriptures that teach the depravity of man and the tragic results of that depravity. One such verse is Isaiah 64:6, which teaches that all our righteousness is filthy rags. The picture that Scriptures paint is not a pretty one. The only works we can produce are as valueless as dung and disgusting, ceremoniously unclean garments. The unbelievers drag these works up before the Great White Throne. It is no wonder that in the process they fall on their knees confessing before the glorious and righteous judge.

Why?

The Bible does not record for us the answer to the question. Why would anyone subject himself or herself to that judgment? Why would anyone face the outer darkness, an eternity without Christ? Could any one of us be the reason why? Is there a person we have not told? Have not loved enough? Have not prayed for? Are we the reason why?

Perhaps you can tell me. Do you have a reason why you will not choose to place your faith in the forgiving God? Time is running out! All of the signs of the coming prince have occurred. The false messiahs, WW I and WW II, the establishment of the nation of Israel in 1948 and the recapture of the city of Jerusalem in 1967 are all behind us. The Islamic nations are poised and ready to strike, to begin the Ezekiel 38 war. The economic and political conditions are right for the institution of the dreaded *"mark of the beast"*. The technology is in place for the entire world to observe the "two witnesses" at one time.

Remember playing "Hide and Seek"? A simple child's game that employed what are possibly the six most profound words in the English language "Ready or not, Here I come!" Why are you not ready?

NOTES

Chapter One

[1] There are ten major doctrinal areas. Many lists will place <u>Theology</u> proper first, which is the study of God. Others place <u>Bibliology</u> first, which is the study of the Bible. The study of the Holy Spirit, which is called <u>Pneumatology</u>, would logically follow the study of God. Then, to finish the trinity, <u>Christology</u> or the study of Christ would come next.

The study of the doctrine of salvation is called <u>Soteriology</u>. After that, we need to study what the Scriptures teach about man, and that study is called <u>Anthropology</u>. The study of man leads to the study of sin, which is called <u>Harmartiology</u>. Then we naturally need to study Satan, but he comes under the broader category of <u>Angelology</u>, or the study of angels.

Next we study what the Bible teaches us about the church, which is called <u>Ecclesiology</u> and finally we study what the Scriptures teach concerning prophecy, which is <u>Eschatology</u>, or literally the study of last things. I personally believe that we need to add the discipline *Israelology* a study of the scriptural teaching about the nation of Israel, her covenants and her future, and show how she is distinct from the church.

[2] The phrase "caught up" is translated in the Latin Vulgate with the word *rapiemur*. From that word we derive the English word *rapture*.

[3] In Hosea 6:3 we read *"Let us know. Let us pursue the knowledge of the Lord. His going forth is established as the morning; He will come to us like the rain, like the latter and former rain to the earth."* The rain falls upon the land of Israel in two seasons. And the Lord comes to the land of Israel on two occasions.

[4] Jeremiah 30:7 speaks about the time of Jacob's trouble. In Daniel 12:1, the trouble is described as *"such as never was since there was a nation."* The Hebrew word for trouble is (צור) tsor. The earliest translation of the Hebrew Scriptures into the Greek language is called the Septuagint and it translates the Hebrew word tsor with the Greek word (φλιπσις), philipses.

The word philipses is translated to the English word tribulation in Matthew 24:29. This horrific period is described for us in Matthew 24:15-26. At the end of that period of time, called the tribulation, those who were killed in those days will need to be raised or *resurrected*.

Many confuse that post-tribulation resurrection with the rapture, when the church is raised.

[5] Rapid Eye Movement

[6] "Jesus Is Coming Soon," original release: 1982, Clifty Records. Available through Acappella Company.

[7] "Big Brother or Mark of the Beast?", by Becky Blanton-Sierra Times.com

Chapter Two

[1] In the parable of the wheat and the tares the harvest is to take place at the "*end of the age*". The Disciples of Jesus asked him to explain "*the end of the age*" as an introduction to the discourse of Matthew 24. The drag net judgment of Matthew 13:47-50 also takes place at the "*end of the age.*" In both parables the angels take all the unbelievers away for judgment and the believers are left on the earth. Matthew 13:49 reads " *the angels will come forth, separate the wicked from among the just...*" The wicked are severed away from the just. Or as we see in Matthew 24 at the end of the tribulation the unbeliever is taken away.

[2] These words from Matthew 25 are often used to encourage Christian charity. Technically the passage refers to the way believers treat the Jewish people during the great tribulation.

[3] There are three basic positions in regards to when the rapture of the church will take place. Some believe the church will not be raptured until the end of the tribulation; that view is called the post-tribulation position. Some believe in a mid-tribulation rapture. And of course, the Scriptures teach a pre-tribulation rapture. The Scriptures teach that the church will be raptured prior to the start of the tribulation.

[4] In 606 B.C., the emperor of Babylon, Nebuchadnezzar, came into Jerusalem. He took many of the elders and potential leaders back into Babylon. Daniel was in this group. Nebuchadnezzar returned 19 years later and took the rest of Jerusalem and Judah into captivity. According to Jeremiah 29:10, the captivity was to last 70 years. Many of the Jewish people elected never to return to their homeland. The book of Esther deals with those Jews who decided not to return. Those who did go back to Israel return in four waves. The earliest being 545 B.C. with the final group returning in 445 B.C., bringing an end to the Babylonian captivity.

⁵ The first was Cyrus' decree in 538 B.C. (2 Chron.36:22-23; Ezra 1:1-4; 5:13). The second was the decree of Darius I (522-486B.C.) in 520 B.C. (Ezra 6:1, 6-12). This decree actually was a confirmation of the first decree. The third was the decree of Artaxerxes Longimanus (464-424) in 457 B.C. (Ezra 7:11-26).

The first two decrees pertain to the rebuilding of the temple in Jerusalem and the third relates to finances for animal sacrifices at the temple. These three say nothing about the rebuilding of the city itself. Since an unwalled city was no threat to a military power, a religious temple could be rebuilt without jeopardizing the military authority of those granting permission to rebuild it.

The start of Daniel's prophecy is a decree that has to do with the rebuilding of the wall. Also, that decree was the fourth decree by Artaxerxes Longimanus, issued on what would correspond to our March 5, 444 B.C. (Nehemiah. 2:1-8). On that occasion Artaxerxes granted the Jewish people permission to rebuild Jerusalem's city walls. This is the same one referred to in Daniel 9:25.

⁶ Biblical prophecy is recorded in Biblical terminology. Biblical years are lunar years, containing 360 days each. The calendar we keep records history in terms of solar years, which include 365 days each. To calibrate a Biblical prophecy fulfilled in our historical calendar requires the conversion of lunar years into solar years.

The process of conversion is to multiply the prophetic years times 360 to determine the length of days in the prophecy. Then, to take that total and divide it by 365 to determine how many solar years are being referred to. The arithmetic would look like this. Seven weeks or 7 x 7 = 49 lunar years. 49 lunar years x 360= 17,640 total days. 17,640 days ÷ 365 = 48.32 solar years. Add that to the starting year of 445 B.C. and the first stage of the prophecy will be completed in the year 396 B.C.

⁷ The word canon means rule and it refers to the standard by which various ancient manuscripts were determined to be included as recognized authentic Bible books. In our literature canon refers to the actual Scriptures when it is used as a noun.

⁸ The first two segments of the prophecy ran consecutively. They total 483 lunar years. The total number of days in the first two phases of the prophecy is 173,880.

476 solar years contain 173,740 days. The 476 solar years will contain 116 extra days for a leap year every fourth year minus the centennial years which are not leap years, however, the 400th year is.

The total number of transpired days is now 173,856. That leaves 24 days left over. Those twenty four days will take the length of the prophecy from March 5, 444 B.C. to March 30, 33 A.D. *(There is only one year from −1 B.C. to +1 A.D.)*

⁹ The Hebrew is פסח (pesah) and is translated Passover. The Jewish people had been enslaved in the land of Egypt for four hundred years, but the Lord raised up

161

Moses and sent him to confront Pharaoh. To encourage Pharaoh to let the Jewish people go, God brought ten plagues upon the land of Egypt. The final plague was death of the first-born.

The Jewish people were instructed to put the lamb's blood on the doorposts of their homes. God said in Exodus 12:12-13 "For I will pass through the land of Egypt on that night, and will strike all the firstborn in the land of Egypt, both man and beast; and against all the gods of Egypt I will execute judgment: I am the Lord. Now the blood shall be a sign for you on the houses where you are. And when I see the blood, I will pass over you; and the plague shall not be on you to destroy you when I strike the land of Egypt."

[10]

Hebrew Month	Our Calendar	Hebrew Month	Our Calendar
1. Tishri	Sept. – Oct.	7. Nisan	March – April
2. Heshvan	Oct. – Nov.	8. Iyar	April – May
3. Kislev	Nov. – Dec.	9. Sivan	May – June
4. Tevet	Dec. – Jan.	10. Tamuz	June – July
5. Shvat	Jan. – Feb.	11. Av	July – August
6. Adar	Feb. – March	12. Elul	Aug. – Sept.

[11] Josephus, "Wars of the Jews", Book VI, chapter 9:3 and the Babylonian Talmud Pesahim 61A.

[12] In Genesis, the description of each of the first six days of creation is concluded with the phrase *"and there was evening and morning,"* therefore the day begins at sundown.

[13] Today the Jewish people skip the one-day Passover feast. They instead celebrate the Feast of Unleavened Bread for eight days beginning on the 15th of Nisan and call it the Passover. The reason they celebrate this way is that the Temple is in ruins and they are not permitted to sacrifice outside of the Temple. Since Passover calls for the slaying of lambs, they cannot celebrate Passover on the proper day.

[14] Seder means "order." It refers to the order of the prayers, the readings and special foods that are eaten during the night to commemorate the exodus from Egypt.

[15] The tray, that contains the three pieces of matzo, is called an echad אחד holder. The undying watchword of the Jewish faith is called the great Shima. It is simply the recitation of the Hebrew of Deuteronomy 6:4. The English reads, *"Hear, O Israel: the*

Lord our God, the Lord is one." The word translated "one" is the Hebrew word Echad which, technically, does not mean one. It is better translated with the term unity. It is the same word translated "one" in Genesis 2:24 where the two (husband and wife) become one flesh. Echad refers to a plurality. At the Passover, the three matzo are a unity reflecting the triunity of God.

[16] Since the Seder is conducted in Jewish homes and not in the Synagogue, Dads become rabbis and need to conduct the lenthy religious service. Books to assist them have been published called haggadas. The word haggadah comes from the Hebrew of Exodus 13:8 where we read והגדת which in English is translated to *"and you shall tell your sons."* The haggadah includes the prayers, the stories, the recipes and the instructions necessary to conduct the Passover Seder.

[17] Each participant at the Passover would partake of a cup of wine four times throughout the Seder. Each time they drink the cup they commemorate one of the promises God gave in Exodus 6:6-7. *"I will bring you out from under the burdens of the Egyptians, I will rescue you from their bondage, and I will redeem you with an outstretched arm and with great judgments. I will take you as My people and I will be your God."*

[18] The first five books of the Scriptures, and selected readings from the writings and the prophets with a commentary from the rabbinic writings.

[19] The middle wall of partition in Greek is "mesotoicon". It refers to a six-foot high stone wall that stood on the Temple mount separating the court of the Gentiles. To go beyond the wall would be penalized by death for the Gentile. The Jewish people were also distinct from the Gentile in their relationship to the law.

[20] "The Chumash, the Stone edition." Comment on Leviticus 23:15-21

[21] "A Guide to Jewish Religious Practice," by Isaac Klein. Distributed by KTAV publishing house. Pg.147

[22] In Hebrew, the imperative verb is a shortened form of the imperfect tense and has the same force as the English imperative. The imperative reflects the will of the speaker.

[23] The indicative mood simply conveys the reality of an action. The imperative mood communicates a command as in the expression "You will go to the store". In the indicative mood this would be a prophetic statement. In the imperative mood could be translated as "You, go to the store!"

[24] "A Guide to Religious Practice," published by the Jewish Theological Seminary of America, 1979, New York. Page 180.

[25] There were *daily* sacrifices brought for personal sins; there was a *weekly* sacrifice brought by the head of the family for the extended household; the head of

each tribe would bring a sacrifice *each month* for the atonement of the sins of each tribe; *once a year* the high priest would enter the Holy of Holies and there, on the Day of Atonement, he would make atonement for himself, his household and then for the entire nation of Israel.

The less frequently the sacrifice was offered, the more expensive the sacrifice and the more people it covered. They all set the stage for a once for all and forever sacrifice of extremely precious material that covers the entire race of mankind.

[26] In Hosea 5:15, the word for affliction is the Hebrew word צור (tsur). It is the word that comes into Yiddish as "tsoris" which means trouble. In Jeremiah 30:7 we see this same word in relation to the great tribulation. Jeremiah refers to the tribulation as *"the time of Jacob's trouble."*

[27] Yom Kippur is literally The Day of Atonement. The Hebrew word for day is Yom (יום) The word translated "atonement" is really in the plural. It is כפרים kipporim. We transliterate kipporim and then change it into a singular form to arrive at the word kippur.

[28] The word translated "shortly come to pass" is the Greek word "tachos". In Acts 12:7 it is translated "suddenly". It doesn't promise that the things will occur soon, so much as when they begin happen they will happen in a rapid succession.

[29] In his commentary on Revelation, Lehman Strauss suggests the following:

Ephesus	Spiritually strong Apostolic	33 -160A.D.
Smyrna	Persecuted Church	160 - 312 A.D.
Pergamos	Religious compromise	313 - 600 A.D.
Thyatira	A woman versus Scripture	600 - 1517
Sardis	Those who escape	1517 - 1750 A.D.
Philadelphia	The open door	1750 - 1950A.D.
Laodicea	Immature and lacking zeal	1950 - to rapture

[30] 1 Corinthians 15:52 reads, *"in a moment"*. The Greek word translated moment is "atomo", which would be the smallest particle of time.

[31] Colossians 1:16, In Isaiah 14:12-14 Lucifer boasts that he would raise his throne above that of the Messiah. It is a false prophecy and in no way proves that he, or any other angel ever sat on a throne.

³² In Revelation 3:5 white raiment is promised as a reward to the ones who overcome. They will also not be blotted out of the book of life. It appears that they receive the white raiment in heaven (Revelation 3:18). In 6:11 we see those who were martyred early in the tribulation are given white raiment. In Revelation 7:9 we see an uncountable multitude from all nations in white raiment. In verses 14-17 it is obvious that these believers have suffered persecution during the tribulation and received their white raiment in heaven.

In 15:6 those wearing white linen are referred to as angels. However, these angels are really men. The word angel also means messenger. There are created beings called angels, but the ones clothed in white linen are men. In 17:1 one of the seven angels begins to function as a messenger by revealing further things to John. In 19:10 John prostrates himself in worship of the messenger who proceeds to identify himself as a man.

³³ 1 Thessalonians 1:10, *"To wait for His Son from heaven...who delivers us from the wrath to come"* The word for *"delivers"* is in Greek "ruomai". That word has the sense of drawing something towards you. It is a beautiful picture of the rapture as the believers of the church age are delivered from the wrath to come by meeting the Lord in the air. The word translated *from* is the Greek word "ek". That word when used with the genitive case has the sense of out from. The word wrath is in the genitive case. So by being drawn by Jesus at the rapture we are delivered out from the wrath to come.

Chapter Three

¹ Remember, this whole discussion takes place in the Jewish capitol, in front of the Jewish Temple, between the Jewish Messiah and His Jewish followers. We would expect the terminology to be understood within a Jewish context. The term Christ in Greek, "Cristos," is a translation of the Hebrew word משיח which we transliterate to Messiah. The term means an anointed one. It refers to all prophets, kings and priests who, through the ceremony of being anointed with oil, received the appointment to their official position.

² "Tables Turned" William Wordsworth 1798

³ "The 1990 Almanac" (Information Please) page 409.

⁴ We are to demolish all theories and every high system of ethics or philosophy set forth to deny the knowledge of God - like the philosophy of Associationism; and then to focus on the truth (Philippians 4:8). Since we are commanded to do so, then we must be able to do so and are responsible for controlling our own thoughts.

Are We There Yet?

[5] A geometric ratio is a progression by multiplication. One becomes three, three becomes nine, nine becomes twenty-seven, etc. An arithmetic ratio is a progression by addition. One becomes four, four becomes seven, seven becomes ten, etc.

[6] "Pogrom is a Russian word that comes from two words meaning after and thunder. The word means riot or storm. It refers to events in pre-war Russia when the czars promoted open violence upon unarmed Jewish citizens.

[7] "The Protocols of the Elders of Zion" was a phony document that alleged itself to be the secret minutes of the first Zionist council. The publications invented a Jewish conspiracy for world domination.

[8] Nietzsche came to pessimistic conclusions that were based on his observations of Christian theology. He apparently studied Christian behavior and Christian theology and found them to be in contradiction. He did not study the Bible and it was never referenced in his work.

We need to turn frequently to the powerful, life-giving word of God. If we do not continually return for fresh illumination from the once and only revelation then our theology can in time grow to become a dead philosophy rather than a living faith.

[9] Niccolo Machiavelli was an administrator and a diplomat who was ousted from power in 1512. He at that time, wrote "The Prince". It has come to be known as the world's most famous master plan for seizing and holding power. The disturbing thing is that his principles are considered in board meetings of Christian organizations.

[10] Nietzsche died before completing a work called "The Will to Power". His sister, Elizabeth, completed the work and added in her own strong nationalistic and anti-Semitic beliefs. This work was later used by the Nazis to wrongly connect Nietzsche with Hitler. Nietzsche may have influenced the Nazis but certainly would not have agreed with them.

[11] The term originally employed by Nietzsche was *"overman,"* Nietzsche's metaphor for the stronger species, the higher type that would be the product of an inevitable counter movement.

[12] Universalists began in 1770, a bit too early for our chart. As the name suggests they believe in universal salvation.

[13] The Disciples of Christ was the product of four men, Barton Stone, Thomas Campbell and his son Alexander, and Walter Scott. They stressed unity over theology and would call themselves 'conservative, God centered, Christ centered and Bible Centered". However, faith is a matter of individual conviction and there was no central authority to establish what is truth and what is heresy.

[14] The belief is that those who have died are waiting for resurrection and judgement in an unconscious state.

[15] Rosicrucians are members of a mystical society founded in the 16th century by Christian Rosenkreuz. Their theology and practices were drawn from the religions of ancient Egypt and combined with Catholicism. The founder lived to be 106 and the society did not last much longer.

[16] The 1990 "Information Please Almanac," page 439.

[17] In John 8:24 the word *"He"* is in italics signifying that the word doesn't appear in the Greek language. Jesus simply said, *"if you believe not that I am"*. The use of the verb (to be) in the first person is a reference to the Tetragrammaton. The Tetragrammaton is the four Hebrew consonants used to represent the Holy name of God יהוה or as they are transliterated into English YHVH. The Tetragrammaton is a form of the verb "to be". The English version translates it LORD.

The phrase *"I am"* is a clear claim to be God and John 8:24 is a clear teaching that the deity of Jesus is a doctrine that must be embraced for salvation. Jesus uses the phrase again in John 8:28 and many Jewish people believed in Him. He used the expression again in John 8:58 and the Jewish people who did not believe in Him picked up stones to stone Him for blasphemy.

[18] The word translated "Lord" is the Greek word "κυριοσ". The Septuagint uses the word to translate the Tetragrammaton. The Apostle Paul uses the Septuagint version of the Scriptures. He would only use "κυριοσ" if he wanted to teach the Deity of Jesus.

[20] The word Talmud means student. It refers to the Jewish oral law. The theory is that when God gave Moses the written law at Mt. Sinai, He whispered the oral interpretation into Moses' ear. Moses told it to Aaron and Aaron told his sons. The oral law continued to be delivered from generation to generation alongside of the written law of Moses which is called the Torah.

After the first century of the Common Era the oral law was transcribed. The Talmud consists of two sections - the Mishna, which is the oral law and the Gemorra, which is commentary on the Mishna. They combine to form a library about twice the size of a standard encyclopedia.

[21] Zohar literally means *"book of splendor"*. It is the chief work of the mystical writings of the Jewish people called the Kaballah. The Zohar is a compilation of short midrashic statements, long homilies and numerous discussions on various topics. The greater part of the Zohar is purported to be the utterances of Simeon Ben Yohai, a second century contributor to the Mishna.

The Zohar first appears in 14th century Spain and is probably the work of Moses de Leon who died in 1305.

[21] The Boston Talmud society published an English version of the Babylonian Talmud in twelve volumes. In the first volume there is a historical section that refers to the followers of Jesus as many and notable persons who were closely aligned with the Pharisees. These early Jewish believers are called both Messiahists and Messianists by the Talmud.

[22] There are some 200,000 variant readings that occur in some 10,000 places in the New Testament. It sounds horrific, but in reality it's all good. The more the variant readings, the more evidence that is available for comparison and contrast to enable the textual critic to establish the Bible text.

Still, the mention of a large number of variants can leave a wrong impression. Westcott and Hort estimated that only about one-eighth of all the variants had any weight and most of them are merely mechanical matters such as spelling or style. Of the whole, then, only about one-sixtieth rise above trivialities. Mathematically that would compute to a text that is 98.33 percent pure, regardless of the text one selects.

[23] An autograph is something written by ones own hand. The term refers to an original manuscript of a Bible text.

[24] The term Hermeneutics comes from ερμηνευω, which means interpret. It is the study of the principles of Biblical interpretation.

[25] In the phrase *"beginning of sorrows"* the word sorrows, ωδινεσ, is literally birth pangs. Many have understood that expression to refer to the beginning of the tribulation. The birth pangs refer to the famines and earthquakes, which occur in the tribulation period. The other events, the appearance of the false messiahs and the world-wide conflicts, have already begun to transpire in the end of the church age.

Philo (20 B.C.-A.D 50), a wealthy Alexandrian Jewish Philosopher who was the most prolific writer of the Hellenistic Jewish position, saw birth pangs as a reference to the rhythmic waves of contractions. To him the birth pangs were up and down shakings much like the tremor experienced in an earthquake. Philo wrote from a zealously secular, non-rabbinical Jewish perspective. His Jewish opposites were the highly religious scribes of the Qumran community. They saw birth pangs as referring to the prelude to the Messianic age.

[26] On two occasions Elisha is seen working miracles in the midst of a famine, in 2 Kings 4:38 and in 2 Kings 6:25. These incidents occur in the same geographical area and are close enough in time to be referring to the same famine.

[27] The twelve tribes of Israel were united under Kings Saul, David and Solomon. After 960 B.C. the ten northern tribes split forming the nation of Israel, whose capitol was Samaria.

²⁸ The term Midrash comes from the Hebrew word d'rash דרש, which means "to search". The term refers both to a style of communication and a set of commentaries. As a communication method, Midrashic literature are stories, legends, tales and anecdotes. The Midrash is also a set of commentaries written in Aramaic and Hebrew, which first appeared in print between 100 and 300 AD.

²⁹ The Hebrew word יום, yom) is translated "day". When it does not mean a literal 24hour period, it refers to a period of time of indefinite length that includes a specific continuous activity. Isaiah 34:8 shows the events that are called the *"day of the Lord"* are both local (34:5-6) and last longer then one day (34:10).

In Jeremiah 46:10, the location has changed from Bozrah in Edom to the North country by the Euphrates. In Ezekiel 13:3-5, the day of the Lord deals with the prophets of Israel, while in Ezekiel 30:4-5 the day of the Lord moves to Egypt, which shows that there are several different events referred to as the day of the Lord. The final day of the Lord, is universal and of indefinite length.

³⁰ Tel is a Semitic word for an artificial mound formed by the overlaying debris of ancient cities, each of which has been built on top of preceding civilizations. Such mounds are found in many regions of the Middle East.

³¹ Antiquities 9:222-227

³² Dispensationalism is a system of interpretation that recognizes different responsibilities assigned to the people of God during different ages. The people of God are always saved by grace through faith. Dispensationalism maintains a consistently literal approach to interpretation and recognizes a distinction between the church and Israel.

³³ In Leviticus 25:3-5 and Leviticus 26:34, Israel is commanded to not sow in the land every seventh year. They were commanded to give the land a Sabbath rest. After four hundred and ninety years of disobedience, the land was entitled to a total of seventy years of rest. Jeremiah 25:9-14 explains how the land will enjoy the rest she is entitled to while the Jewish people are in the Babylonian captivity.

³⁴ There is no year zero and so we add one year to our calculation and the nine additional months is ¾ of a second year or three months short of two years.

Chapter Four

¹ There is one Greek word that is translated by the English phrase, *"one possessed by a devil"* The word is δαιμονζομενος (daimonzomenos). It would better be transliterated "demonized". People have been teaching that Christians can be demon obsessed, but not demon possessed. The New Testament does not teach anything about

demon possession or demon obsession, but that whoever serves sin becomes a slave to sin. The degree to which a person submits to evil is the degree to which the demons will have influence over him (John 8:34, Romans 6:16)

[2] This phrase begins with μητι (Mhti) That word is untranslatable, and precedes questions where the answer is in doubt. The crowd could not confer Messianic credentials upon Jesus without the approval of the ruling Pharisees. However, they certainly recognized the uniqueness of the signature miracle and were looking to the Pharisees to concur officially.

[3] The word translated world (αιωνι aiwni) would be better translated age. The Greek word (κοσμοσ kosmos) is more strictly our word for world

[4] Generation is a translation of γενεα (genea). In Luke 21:32 and in Matthew 24:34 Jesus says that this generation shall not pass till all these things be fulfilled. In neither verse is the word generation referring to the people of the time, but rather the people of that kind. The word generation in the gospels is always referring to the Jewish people. The Jewish people will survive regardless of how severe the persecution against them becomes.

[5] A quote from Palm 118:26 ברך הבה בשם יהוה Baruch Habah Bashem Adonoi.

[6] The groom gives his bride a contract called a ketuvah, literally a writing. In it he promises to care and provide for her. The wedding pictures the relationship that the believer has with the Lord. God makes all the promises to us and we merely receive them by faith.

[7] The first of these burdens is the burden of Babylon in Isaiah 13 and the language clearly has a dual reference to events that take place in the great tribulation in verses 9-13.

The burden of Moab is discussed in Isaiah 15. The geographical locations mentioned could easily have a dual reference to end time events, but in this chapter it is only speculative.

The next is the burden of Damascus in Isaiah 17, which we are now discussing. The burden of Egypt is in Isaiah 19: 19-25 where alliances that will only occur in the millennial kingdom are discussed.

In Isaiah 21 we see the burdens of the desert, Dumah and Arabia. Again, the language is unspecific but could easily have a dual view; both immediate and end time perspective. In Isaiah 22 the burden of the Valley of Vision is discussed, and the people on the housetops in 22:1 could refer to the flood of Matthew 24 and Revelation 12. In 22:22 the key to the house of David and the open door of Revelation 3:8 are mentioned.

In Isaiah 23 the burden of Tyre is discussed and the chapter skips from the siege under Nebuchadnezzar to the destruction under Alexander the Great and then to the peace under the rule of the Messiah in the millennial reign.

[8] A Sanskrit or Aryan word meaning "the sea coast" Also one of the sons of Javan (Genesis 10:4, 1 Chronicles 1:7); in Hebrew תרשיש. The name of a place of unknown certainty mentioned first at the time of Solomon. There were probably several different cities of the same name, which were located on a seacoast. The term, *"young lions,"* refers to colonies. Spain, Portugal and Britain all produced colonies.

[9] Jerome identified Magog as referring to the Scythian nations, fierce and innumerable, who live beyond the Caucasus and Lake Maeotis near the Caspian Sea and spread onward to India.

[10] Aarmagedon literally means "mount of Megiddo". Located on the south side of the valley of Megiddo, or Esdraelon, southwest of Mount Carmel (2 Chr. 35:22, Zech. 12:11). Megiddo was the capital of a portion of Canaan that was given to Joshua (Josh 12:21, 17:11, Jud. 1:27).

It is at the entrance to a pass across the Carmel mountain range, on the main highway between Asia and Africa and is the key position between the Euphrates and the Nile. Because of its strategic location, many battles have been waged there throughout the centuries. The anti Christ will gather the troops together there for the final assault on the Jewish people.

[11] The word translated *"captivity"* in Zechariah 14:2, ☐☐ (Gowlah), is an active participle and has a simple reference to being carried away. When the Lord stands at the mount of Olives, half the city will be carried away and removed.

[12] The Stone edition of the Chumash, Leviticus 26:41.

[13] Ibid page 717

[14] Ibid.

[15] The time from 516 B.C. to 70 A.D. would only be 585 total years since there is no year zero.

[16] The number of years from the destruction of Jerusalem under Rome in the year 70 until the establishment of the modern nation of Israel in 1948.

Chapter Five

[1] The context of 2 Thessalonians 2 is established as our gathering together unto the Lord. In verse 3, tapterhere is a reference to a "falling away". The word from which we get apostasy is the word for falling away.

That there will be an end time departure from the faith is certain from 1 Timothy 4:1-3 and 2 Timothy 3:1-6. Those passages are probably referring to some of the results of the teachings of the false Messiah's that Jesus mentions.

The Greek word "apostocia" is almost always understood as a departure from the faith. However, the word truly just means a departure, and the context here is our gathering together to meet the Lord. The definite article added to the word could easily be referring to **the** rapture of the Church. The next several verses describe how the removal of the restrainer is necessary, since the restrainer is the Holy Spirit and since He will never leave us or forsake us, when He departs we depart with Him and so shall we be with the Lord.

[2] The Tribulation is thought of as being universal. Since it is the time of Jacob's trouble, the events of the tribulation are primarily of a local concern. The seal judgments that open the tribulation only affect $1/4^{th}$ of the world (Revelation 6:8). The 144,000 are selected from the twelve tribes, referring to Biblical territory in the land of Israel. The trumpet judgments of Revelation 8 only deal with $1/3^{rd}$ of the world. The bowl judgments are a reiteration of the trumpets only with the whole Roman world in view.

[3] A horn represents a king. (Daniel 8:21,Revelation 17:7-11)

[4] The great words are mentioned in Daniel 7:20, 25; 11:36 and Revelation 13:5.

[5] The word for wear out is "bela," a Chaldee word meaning afflict. The Hebrew word for affliction is translated "tribulation".

[6] In Mesopotamian thinking, "the times" are governed by cosmic decrees embodied in the "Tablets of Destinies". These tablets are normally entrusted to either the assembly of the gods or to the head of the pantheon. In a number of ancient tales they are misappropriated. In "Enuma Elish Kingu," Tiamat's sidekick has them. In "The Anzu Myth," a monster, Anzu, stole them and threatened to use them, putting everything in the universe in jeopardy.

[7] Antiochus Epiphanies is the Syrian ruler who organized the expedition against Jerusalem that resulted in the revolt of the Maccabees. That revolt and subsequent

success of the heroic gorilla warfare of the Jewish people is the background behind the holiday of Hanukkah.

[8] Epiphanies means illustrious.

[9] The King James Version

[10] The Hebrew word for land and earth is eratz ארץ. I t should read "from the land", meaning the land of Israel. John is writing in Greek, but the Revelation is coming from the Hebrew God to a Hebrew prophet and we should expect to see Hebrew idioms employed.

[11] The whole world wondered after the first beast before the second beast even appears on the scene (Revelation 13:3) The first beast is given power over the Gentiles (Revelation 13:7) before the second beast appears.

[12] "The Illustrated Bible Dictionary", by Tyndale House Publishers. Volume 2, page 925.

[13] Some hypothesize that Dan is missing because Dan was the first tribe to enter into idolatry (Judges 18:30). However, Dan is mentioned in the millennial list in Ezekiel 48:2. There seems to be little to explain Dan's disqualification and if Dan was disqualified during the tribulation, under what circumstances was the tribe reinstated for the kingdom?

[14] The northern kingdom is called Ephraim in Isaiah, which is the other tribe that is missing in the list of the 144,000.

[15] The Greek word for soul is ψυχη,(psuecha). In the Septuagint Psuecha most often translates the Hebrew word נפש, (nefesh) The word, Nefesh, is used in Genesis for animals and fish.

[16] Of the pit of the abyss (του φρεατος τ| σ αβυσσου]). □βυσσος (Abussos) is an old adjective and βυθος (buthos) depth, without depth but □ □βυσσος hē abussos supply ÷ωρα (chōra) place, the bottomless place. It occurs in Rom. 10:7 for the common receptacle of the dead for Hades (Sheol), but in Luke 8:31 a lower depth is for the abode of demons and, in this sense, it occurs in Rev. 9:1, 2, 11; 11:7; 17:8; 20:1, 3

[17] It is a bit involved comparing Matthew 28, Mark 16, Luke 24 and John 20. With a bit of work the four accounts reconcile rather nicely. There are at least two angels and two groups of women. One group entered the tomb and then ran and told the disciples. A second group, upon seeing the angel outside the tomb, fled and did not say anything (Mark 16:8). One angel sat outside the tomb on the stone and addressed the woman outside. He then entered the tomb with a second angel and addressed the women inside.

Chapter Six

[1] This concept is mentioned 13 times in the Scriptures 4 times in the Old Testament (Exodus 32:32, 33, Psalms 69:28 and Daniel 12:1) and 9 times in the New Testament (Luke10:20; Philippians 4:3; Revelation 3:5; 13:8; 17:8; 20:11-12, 15, 22; 18-19).

[2] There are two different Greek words translated "book"; Biblion (Biblion) and Biblo~ (Biblos). Both are used in the phrase "book of life". Biblion (Biblion) in Revelation 13:8; 17:8, 20:12 and 21:27 and Biblo~ (Biblos) in Philippians 4:3, Revelation 3:5 and 20:15. However, names are never blotted out of Biblion (Biblion) (Revelation 21:27).

[3] Every believer will stand before the judgment seat of Christ (1 Corinthians 3:13-15, 2 Corinthians 5:10 and Romans 14:11). This is not the Great white throne. In Revelation 20:11, Christ sits on a throne (qrono~), not the Bhmato~ (Bamatos) seat of 2 Corinthians 5:10. At the great white throne all are lost; at the judgment seat of Christ all are saved. The judgment seat of Christ is where believers' works are examined and either rewarded or burned up.

[4] What does the term second death mean? Death is the end of life. Eternal life is the knowledge of God and Jesus Christ (John 17:3). These before the throne know Jesus and see Him in His glorious splendor. They fall on their knees, they worship Him and then, having become alive spiritually, they will be cast from Jesus eternally. They will die a second death. They will return to the lost condition of being separated from God.